THE DESERT

LITERATURE OF THE AMERICAN WILDERNESS

The Peregrine Smith Literature of the American Wilderness series is designed to make available the outstanding natural history writings of the North American continent from the first settlements and discoveries to the present day. All volumes in the series will feature uniform attractive designs and modest prices to enable all readers to add these beautiful volumes to their library. Outstanding new introductions by noted scholars, poets and wilderness writers will enhance readers' understanding of these classic volumes celebrating the beauty and wonder of the American earth and experience.

Editorial advisers to the series are William Howarth of Princeton University, and Frank Bergon of Vassar College.

Titles in print:

John Muir, *Wilderness Essays*. Edited with an introduction and notes by Frank Buske.

Henry David Thoreau, *The Natural History Essays*. Edited with an introduction and notes by Robert Sattelmeyer.

John C. Van Dyke, *The Desert*. Introduction by Richard Shelton.

Forthcoming titles:

William Byrd, *History of the Dividing Line*. Edited with an introduction and notes by Robert Peck.

John Burroughs, *Selections* from his natural history writing. Edited with an introduction and notes by Frank Bergon.

Henry David Thoreau, *The Journal*, all fourteen volumes to be published for the first time volume by volume in a handsome paperback set. Introductions by Walter Harding.

JOHN C. VAN DYKE

THE DESERT

➜

Peregrine Smith, Inc.

SALT LAKE CITY

1980

LITERATURE OF THE AMERICAN WILDERNESS

Introduction copyright © 1980 by Peregrine Smith, Inc.

Library of Congress Cataloging in Publication Data

Van Dyke, John Charles, 1856-1932.
    The desert.

    (Literature of the American wilderness)
    Reprint of the 1901 ed. published by Scribner, New York.
        1. Southwest, New—Description and travel. 2. Deserts—Southwest, New. 3. Natural history—Southwest, New. 4. Van Dyke, John Charles, 1856-1932. I. Title.
[F786.V24 1980] 917.9'0954   80-10892
ISBN 0-87905-073-X

Manufactured in the United States of America.

PREFACE-DEDICATION

ᘒ

A. M. C.

After the making of Eden came a serpent,
and after the gorgeous furnishing of the world,
a human being. Why the existence of the destroyers? What monstrous folly, think you,
ever led Nature to create her one great enemy
—man! Before his coming security may have
been; but how soon she learned the meaning of
fear when this new Œdipus of her brood was
brought forth! And how instinctively she
taught the fear of him to the rest of her children! To-day, after centuries of association,
every bird and beast and creeping thing—the
wolf in the forest, the antelope on the plain,
the wild fowl in the sedge—fly from his approach. They know his civilization means their
destruction. Even the grizzly, secure in the
chaparral of his mountain home, flinches as he
crosses the white man's trail. The boot mark

in the dust smells of blood and iron. The great annihilator has come and fear travels with him.

"Familiar facts," you will say. Yes; and not unfamiliar the knowledge that with the coming of civilization the grasses and the wild flowers perish, the forest falls and its place is taken by brambles, the mountains are blasted in the search for minerals, the plains are broken by the plow and the soil is gradually washed into the rivers. Last of all, when the forests have gone the rains cease falling, the streams dry up, the ground parches and yields no life, and the artificial desert—the desert made by the tramp of human feet—begins to show itself. Yes; everyone must have cast a backward glance and seen Nature's beauties beaten to ashes under the successive marches of civilization. The older portions of the earth show their desolation plainly enough, and the ascending smoke and dust of the ruin have even tainted the air and dimmed the sunlight.

Indeed, I am not speaking figuratively or extravagantly. We have often heard of "Sunny Italy" or the "clear light" of Egypt, but believe me there is no sunlight there compared with that which falls upon the upper peaks of

the Sierra Madre or the uninhabitable wastes of
the Colorado Desert. Pure sunlight requires for
its existence pure air, and the Old World has
little of it left. When you are in Rome again
and stand upon that hill where all good romanticists go at sunset, look out and notice how
dense is the atmosphere between you and St.
Peter's dome. That same thick air is all over
Europe, all around the Mediterranean, even
over in Mesopotamia and by the banks of the
Ganges. It has been breathed and burned and
battle-smoked for ten thousand years. Ride up
and over the high table-lands of Montana—one
can still ride there for days without seeing a
trace of humanity—and how clear and scentless,
how absolutely intangible that sky-blown sun-
shot atmosphere ! You breathe it without feeling it, you see through it a hundred miles and
the picture is not blurred by it.

It is just so with Nature's color. True
enough, there is much rich color at Venice, at
Cairo, at Constantinople. Its beauty need not
be denied ; and yet it is an artificial, a chemical
color, caused by the disintegration of matter—
the decay of stone, wood, and iron torn from
the neighboring mountains. It is Nature after
a poor fashion—Nature subordinated to the will

of man. Once more ride over the enchanted
mesas of Arizona at sunrise or at sunset, with
the ragged mountains of Mexico to the south of
you and the broken spurs of the great sierra
round about you ; and all the glory of the old
shall be as nothing to the gold and purple and
burning crimson of this new world.

You will not be surprised then if, in speaking
of desert, mesa and mountain I once more take
you far beyond the wire fence of civilization to
those places (unhappily few now) where the
trail is unbroken and the mountain peak un-
blazed. I was never over-fond of park and
garden nature-study. If we would know the
great truths we must seek them at the source.
The sandy wastes, the arid lands, the porphyry
mountain peaks may be thought profitless
places for pilgrimages ; but how often have you
and I, and that one we both loved so much,
found beauty in neglected marshes, in wintry
forests, and in barren hill-sides ! The love of
Nature is after all an acquired taste. One begins by admiring the Hudson-River landscape
and ends by loving the desolation of Sahara.
Just why or how the change would be difficult
to explain. You cannot always dissect a taste
or a passion. Nor can you pin Nature to a

board and chart her beauties with square and compasses. One can give his impression and but little more. Perhaps I can tell you something of what I have seen in these two years of wandering; but I shall never be able to tell you the grandeur of these mountains, nor the glory of color that wraps the burning sands at their feet. We shoot arrows at the sun in vain; yet still we shoot.

And so it is that my book is only an excuse for talking about the beautiful things in this desert world that stretches down the Pacific Coast, and across Arizona and Sonora. The desert has gone a-begging for a word of praise these many years. It never had a sacred poet; it has in me only a lover. But I trust that you, and the nature-loving public you represent, will accept this record of the Colorado and the Mojave as at least truthful. Given the facts perhaps the poet with his fancies will come hereafter.

JOHN C. VAN DYKE.

LA NORIA VERDE
FEBRUARY, 1901.

INTRODUCTION

In the early summer of 1898, an asthmatic forty-two-year-old university professor-librarian, accompanied by a fox terrier named Cappy, rode an Indian pony out of the Hemet Valley through the San Gorgonio Pass near what is now San Bernardino and headed southeast into the Colorado Desert. He was wearing lightweight clothing and a pair of moccasins he had made from a Sioux pattern. His entire "outfit"—including rifle, pistol, hatchet, shovel, blankets, pans and tin cups, dried food, and one gallon of water—weighed less than fifty pounds; and he was entering a desert so formidable that even the birds who blundered into it rushed on to more hospitable regions.

But this lone traveller, neither young nor in good health, possessed two of the most highly trained mechanisms for visual perception in America—his eyes. He was John C. Van Dyke, art historian and art critic, who had spent much of his life in the finest galleries of Europe, looking, pondering, and returning to look again. He was Professor of Art History at Rutgers University, Librarian of the Sage Library, and the author of two books and several pamphlets on paintings, aesthetic theory, and the theory of visual perception. His books on art theory, *Art for Art's Sake* and *Nature for Its Own Sake*, had been well-received, especially by painters, although his ideas ran counter to some theories of art which were fashionable at the time. He was a disciple of John Ruskin and a friend of many of the best-known painters of his day, including James McNeil Whistler, whose fame has since been somewhat eclipsed by that of his own mother.

When John Van Dyke rode out of the San Gorgonio Pass, he entered one of the greatest art galleries he was ever to see; and he was to live in it for the better part of three years, never ceasing to explore, evaluate, and ruminate while somehow managing to keep himself alive. He wandered back and forth through the Colorado, Sonoran, and Mojave Deserts—vast galleries whose works he examined with the intensity of a lover and the precision of a scientist. During the first year he rode his horse southeast through the blistering Colorado Desert, across the northern Sonoran Desert from west to east, and southward into Mexico, almost to Guaymas. During the next two years he was to range, although not on horseback, as far south as Oaxaca, as far north as Oregon, and as far east as Del Rio, Texas; and he would walk into the Mojave and Death Valley for a stay of several months with only what he could carry on his back and with only his dog for company.

And he paid the price such a desert gallery demands. He suffered from heat, lack of water, and exposure. He suffered from illness, depression, and an unimaginable solitude. But he survived and wrote *The Desert*.

In his autobiography, written more than thirty years later and never published, he recounted that after eight in the morning during that first summer the sand became too hot for the dog to walk on. When the terrier began to howl with pain, Van Dyke would lift him onto the horse where Cappy rode crosswise behind the saddle, leaning against his master's back to keep his balance. "We were an odd combination," Van Dyke comments, "but we pulled together...."

The poet Blake wrote: "If the doors of perception were cleansed, everything would appear to man as it is, infinite." This man who rode through the desert with a dog perched on the horse behind him had spent most of his life trying to see beauty clearly and to see it whole, to cleanse and purify the doors of his perception. And because of that he saw the world of the desert as it was—infinite and infinitely beautiful. In a later book he used the term "sensuous seeing" to describe the way a painter or poet examines the world. It is no wonder then that *The Desert* has been described as a prose poem.

And since the world he saw no longer exists except in the most fragmented, damaged, and moribund condition, it seems almost a miracle that this man, of all others, should have been led by a long chain of curious and often unhappy circumstances to that place at that time, as if he had been sent to record his impressions of the singular beauty about to be destroyed.

He came to the Southwest and ultimately to the desert because of illness, but there is a great discrepancy between his subsequent behavior and any recognized cure for asthma. And there are repeated references in his autobiography which suggest that he later recognized his behavior during those three years for what it probably was— compulsive and out of control. He was on a binge, possibly the greatest binge of his life, an enormous flirtation with death and a love affair with the desert's beauty. He had heard all the horror stories about the desert, knew its dangers, but chose to go into it anyway. "I was just ill enough," he says, "not to care about perils and morbid enough to prefer dying in the sand, alone, to passing out in a hotel with a roommaid weeping at the foot of the bed."

During his wanderings in the desert, he overcame asthma only to fall victim to a severe, continuing fever which he thought to be malaria, but which might have been any of several diseases aggravated by his constant exertion, deprivation, and exposure. It could have been valley fever, native to the Sonoran Desert. "It seems, as I look back upon that western wandering, that I never got any rest. I did the wrong thing, and persisted in it, month after month, with the result that I got worse instead of better. Apparently I was as tough as a gray wolf and could run the mountains day and night. But fever was running with me."

Whatever the fever was, he survived it and later spoke of it with less bitterness than he did the Eastern doctors who, he said, "cut a perfectly good appendix out of me" resulting in "postoperative pnemonia." And he survived even that to live to the age of seventy-six, travel, teach, and write several more books. He was obviously a vigorous man. But the desert took its toll. After his three year adventure he returned to his home in New Brunswick, New Jersey, a far different man than the one who had left. "I came back to myself, but in a dull heavy way. After such an illness in middle life, one is never young again." Before that, in the Preface to *The Desert* he had referred to himself as "only a lover." And his

affair with the desert was a love affair in the grand
manner, to which he gave himself entirely and for
which he risked his life each day. Judging by his
later books and the autobiography, it was his last
grand affair; and he never married.

Later, he continued to travel and write about
what he observed—books on the West Indies,
Egypt, Java, the American West, and one about
New York City. He edited the memoirs of Andrew
Carnegie and, in 1920, he published an excellent
book on the Grand Canyon after spending a good
deal of time there. But even this, *The Grand Canyon of the Colorado*, lacks the passion and intensity
of *The Desert*. By that time he was older, the
Grand Canyon was swarming with tourists thanks
to the Union Pacific Railroad, and Van Dyke might
well have thought that both beauty and youth
were being wasted on the young. At the end of
the book he admits that the Canyon is beyond his
ability to describe, just as it has never been ade-
quately captured by painters or poets. He con-
cludes that the best description of the Canyon is
probably what most tourists say upon first seeing
it: "Good God!"

The Desert is his masterpiece. Into it he poured
all his passion and sensitivity. It is filled with his
precise observations, his feeling for line, color,
tone, and harmony and all his "sensuous seeing."
In spite of brilliant books on the desert in more

recent years by such writers as Joseph Wood Krutch and Edward Abbey, no one has ever surpassed *The Desert*, not even the poets who have attempted to deal with the landscape through which John Van Dyke wandered as "only a lover." His book is a touchstone, a model of accuracy, deep feeling, and simplicity before which other writers bow.

And it is a book about the desert, not about the man. Van Dyke never intrudes upon his subject. He is merely an observer, although a passionate one, who records, explains, and sometimes comments. The reader who wants an account of the author's adventures—his daily exertions in order to find water, his narrow escapes, his encounters with wolves—will have to look elsewhere and will probably be disappointed at how little Van Dyke chose to record of his life and daily activities during his three years in the desert. All I have been able to find of this material is contained in two chapters of his book *The Open Spaces* (1922) and in two chapters of his unpublished autobiography. A handwritten transcript of the autobiography was made by Robert Mitchell, and to that I am indebted for quotations and information in this Introduction.

During his stay in the desert, Van Dyke's first concern was always for water. He soon trained himself to drink water only at night and in the morning, but both the horse and dog required more water than he did. He learned to be very "cunning" in his quest for water. In some areas of the Colorado Desert, where there was almost no wildlife or vegetation, he learned to follow the direction of doves in flight and sometimes find a trickle of water emerging from the base of a mountain, or a pocket of water in a natural stone basin under an overhang. He learned to dig at the base of any mountain where vegetation suggested the presence of water, and often found it.

"I was quite pleased with my cunning in finding this water in drips and potholes and under dry waterfalls. And the dog and horse grew cunning about it too. When I began digging in the gravel they knew at once that I was after water and would crowd forward with paw and hoof, pushing the gravel into the hole until I had to drive them away with the shovel. They were thirsty and could not disguise the fact."

Of the quality of water he found in these places he says nothing. But it must have been superior to the alternatives. "Once or twice I ran pretty dry and had to slash into a *bisnaga* [barrel cactus] or a sahuaro to get at the wet pulp, but, while that sustained me, the dog and horse would scarcely touch it." He made it a point never to travel more than twenty miles from a source of water. If by then he had not found another source, he would turn back and start out the next day in a different direction.

The desert-bred pony wandered free at night and ate grass which he found in clumps here and there, especially in the mountains. He grazed far afield, but returned to the camp several times each night to make sure Van Dyke and the dog were still there. Once he returned at a gallop in the middle of the night, chased by three gray wolves. When there was no grass he learned to eat the joints of cholla cactus from which Van Dyke had removed the spines. The dog and man lived mostly on rabbit and quail, since the art critic was an excellent shot with both rifle and pistol.

No map of Van Dyke's wandering exists. He had the skills necessary to survive in a hostile region, and he had previously gained considerable experience knocking about in remote areas of the Midwest, Montana, and Canada. But it is also clear that there were times when he had only the vaguest notion of where he actually was. At one point in Sonora, Mexico, he encountered a *rancheria* where, he says, "[I] got my direction and went on." Elsewhere in the autobiography he says: "I had no definite line of travel in mind. I was not an exploring expedition, making no map and keeping no journal. I had not thought of ever writing about the trip. In short, I was just drifting with the wind. But even drifting in Southwestern Arizona I found rather difficult." In *The Open Spaces* he says: "I cannot well remember the exact route of the Odyssey, for I kept no record of my movements. I was not travelling by map." Considering where he was, his mapless condition suggests an enormous faith in himself, God, providence, or all three.

Nevertheless, we know his general route. On the pony, he came down the Coachella Valley and passed through the Salton Sea Basin, which was a desert with almost no vegetation—Imperial Valley was still in the future. He cut across the northeastern corner of Baja, California and encountered the Colorado River at a point near the border between Arizona and Mexico. The Colorado was, at that time, broad and untamed. He searched up and down the river for the best place to cross, built a raft of driftwood and reeds, and ferried his supplies across. He then swam back and swam his pony across. We do not know how the spunky terrier got across—probably on the raft.

Van Dyke then rode north along the river to Yuma from which he travelled almost due east, following the railroad line to Tucson. In Tucson he rested, restocked, and consulted two scientist-professors at the tiny Arizona Territorial University. (Arizona was not to become a state for another thirteen years.) The professors were Robert

H. Forbes, an agricultural chemist, and William P. Blake, a geologist. The fact that he consulted these two specialists suggests that by this time Van Dyke was at least planning to write the book or, as is more likely the case, was already well along with it. Later, Forbes was to help him make corrections between the first and second printings.

From Tucson he travelled roughly south past Baboquivari Peak and crossed the Mexican border considerably west of Nogales. From there he took a long plunge southwest toward Tiburon Island in the Gulf of California. During this stretch he travelled for six weeks without seeing another human being. Much of the time there was no water to be found, and both the horse and dog learned to accept what moisture they could from the cacti Van Dyke cut open. But there was food in abundance. In the autobiography he says: "I found water awful and there were bands of antelope, with much small game everywhere. So the outfit did not suffer but I learned to weary of the sun, and the hot sky, and the lone region. I was studying every phase of the desert and during the heat of the day when I could get in the shadow of a rock wall I was writing my impressions but I was ill and alone and the whole outlook was dreary."

From a point on the Gulf of California near Tiburon Island he turned back inland, riding southeast until he encountered some *rancherias*. In

The Open Spaces Van Dyke describes in lyrical terms the casual hospitality and relaxed atmosphere of the Sonoran *rancheria* before the turn of the century. "The coffeepot and bean-pot were always over the fire and in constant requisition.... When it came to retiring for the night, one simply dragged out a rawhide or canvas cot to whatever part of the premises he pleased, spread his blankets, and went to sleep listening to the dogs chasing coyotes."

He left his horse at the *rancheria* La Noria Verde near Hermosillo and, with the dog, walked until he encountered the railroad line and followed it to Guaymas. He spent the remainder of the winter in Guaymas, hiking each day into the surrounding mountains and Yaqui country to study the plants, animals, and landscape of that part of the Sonoran Desert.

In the early spring he started out again, leaving his horse and "outfit" at the *rancheria,* but taking the dog with him. He went up to Tucson, on to the Grand Canyon where he stayed "a week or more," and then to the Colorado River and across it to Needles, California. We do not know how he travelled during this leg of the journey, but it was probably by train whenever possible. At Needles he made up another "outfit" which he could carry on his back and, with the dog for company, started walking west across the Mojave

Desert. He followed the Santa Fe Railroad line, making large half-circles away from it to study and observe everything he could about the desert. At some point he left the railroad line for good and wandered throughout the desert, spending some time in Death Valley.

His health had begun to deteriorate rapidly, although he did not refer to the problem as "fever" until the end of the summer. "I had been studying the breakdown and pushout of mountains into valleys and flows for many weeks," he said in the autobiography. "And I had been writing about that and a hundred other things as they came up in the desert. The writing was done under difficulties of heat, wind, dust, —done with my back against a rock in a double sense. I was not well and suffered greatly from depression." It was the summer of 1899.

In late summer he left the Mojave and travelled up the San Joaquin Valley—by what means we do not know—eventually going as far north as the Oregon border and crossing it to explore and camp in the Siskiyou Forest. He went from there to El Paso, entered Mexico by train, went on through Chihuahua, Mexico City, and down to Cuautla, where he spent several weeks "under the lee of the volcano Popocatepetl." At this point in the autobiography there is some confusion and the disquieting statement: "Fever had got into my bones." It is clear that he went on to Oaxaca and then to see the Mitla Ruins. "But the fever must have been very high," he says, "and the next week I could remember nothing of what I had seen there." Finally, he decided to return to Guaymas, but he chose a most circuitous route. With Cappy the terrier he "worried around" by El Paso and Nogales and arrived in Guaymas to spend what remained of his second winter since beginning his Western wanderings. In Guaymas he "did a little writing but was not very effective."

At this point his fever was so bad that he decided to return to his home in New Brunswick, New Jersey; but it was to be another year before he did so. Perhaps the fever abated or perhaps he simply decided not to give in to it. At any rate, he returned to Tucson in the spring, spent some time exploring and studying the Santa Rita Mountains, drifted slowly across New Mexico and evidently spent part of the winter in Del Rio, Texas. He mailed the manuscript of *The Desert* to Scribner's from Del Rio in May, 1901,* three years after he had set out on his Indian pony through the San Gorgonio Pass in California. Shortly after that, with Cappy under his arm, he boarded the train for home.

Tracing the path of Van Dyke's wanderings brings into focus the curious question of exactly when the book was written. In *The Open Spaces*, more than twenty years after the fact, Van Dyke says: "The book was written that first summer at odd intervals when I lay with my back against a rock or propped up in the sand." Lawrence Clark Powell quotes this statement in his "Introduction" to the 1976 edition (Arizona Historical Society) and accepts it, but I cannot. The statement is at odds with both the autobiography and the book itself. Van Dyke could not very well have written the book in the summer of 1898 because he did not visit the Mojave until the summer of 1899. And there are clear indications in the autobiography that he continued to work on the book until May of 1901.

The other alternative is that he considered the book finished at the end of the summer of 1898, but later inserted or added information concerning the Mojave. This is a possibility, but would seem negated by the structure of the book itself. Most of the chapters are organized according to a particular subject, such as "Desert Animals," and the observations he made while in the Mojave are well-integrated, suggesting that he did not patch the book together in this way. From a close reading of the autobiography in conjunction with *The Desert*, I must draw the conclusion that he worked on the book during the entire three years of his wanderings, and that as soon as he finished it he mailed it to Scribner's and went home.

But why didn't he go home sooner, sick and exhausted as he was? And why did he go into the desert in the first place? Was it to cure his illness or to write a book, or both? In the autobiography he says, "I had not thought of ever writing about the trip." And in that same document he makes it clear that he realized his exertions in the desert were not improving his health but impairing it. Why then? In later years he must have been asked that question many times and must also often have asked it of himself. In the autobiography he makes several attempts to answer it, none of them entirely satisfactory.

"If asked why I went in there," he says, "I could answer because I was ill but perhaps some animal instinct in me urged me to leave the herd and go off by myself. If asked why I went alone the answer would be again because I was ill and perhaps wanted to be alone, or perhaps it would be truer to say that I could find no one to go with me." Elsewhere in the autobiography he says: "I never tired of the beauty of the desert. Its fiery dawns and orange sunsets, and opalescent air with the grim grandeur of its tall mountains never paled. But I began to long for the sight of familiar faces, and the sound of friendly voices. Still I kept on alone. There seemed no alternative."

That, perhaps, is closest to the answer. "There seemed no alternative." He was in love with the desert, mesmerized by it; and such love affairs are not conducted according to the dictates of logic or even good sense. His research for the book did not hold him in the desert, nor did his failing health cause him to flee. He was in love, and the book is a by-product of that love affair. In that fact lies its power. Beneath all its precise description and accurate information is the half-hidden voice of his complete subjugation, his helplessness in the face of a beauty so powerful that he could not be turned aside by danger, discomfort, or disease. And in the book itself he says: "The weird solitude, the great silence, the grim desolation, are the very things with which every desert wanderer eventually falls in love."

The fact that most of the beauty he described no longer exists is too obvious to be dwelt upon. Seventy years after he wrote his love song to the desert, I wrote a requiem for it. What has happened to it in those seventy years is history, as black and desolating as history can be. His book contains a sharp warning: "The desert should never be reclaimed!" He lived long enough to see reclamation projects well underway in what was to become the Imperial Valley, and today there is, practically speaking, no Colorado Desert left. It is not even named on most maps and few people know where it was.

But Van Dyke did not live long enough to

see the worst. That nightmare is ours. It begins with the bulldozer and runs the full gamut of tract housing, shopping centers, golf courses, trailer parks, and dune buggies. It is swallowing the Sonoran Desert just as agriculture and urbanization swallowed the Colorado Desert. It is spreading daily ever larger out of the towns and cities, a nightmare of our own creation. Where are the herds of antelope Van Dyke spoke of, and the gray wolves, and the pure air?

I have not attempted to analyze the book, nor even discuss it in detail, preferring to let it speak for itself. *The Desert* is what it is and does not need the faint imprimatur of my commentary. By focusing on the author and his wanderings, I have attempted to provide the reader with a context which might help give the book still another dimension. And since my focus is the man, there is one more detail about him I feel I must add. It is a small detail, but salient when seen from a contemporary perspective. During his sojourn in the desert, while Van Dyke was digging so many holes in order to find water, he discovered gold. Not once but several times. He kept no record of where these places were; and thirty years later, in the autobiography, he casually mentions it: "Occasionally I found particles of gold at the bottom..., but that did not greatly interest me. I wasn't seeking gold."

Ultimately, I suppose, it is true that we all find what we are looking for; and the pity is that we are so often looking for the wrong things. John Van Dyke found what he was looking for and it was beautiful. He left his impressions of it for us. We are much in his debt.

Richard Shelton
January, 1980
Tucson

The Desert was an immediate success and has taken its rightful place among a small handful of books as a standard work on the American Desert. It is one of the few books of its kind to be praised for its scientific accuracy while at the same time being called "rhapsodic" and a "prose poem." Originally published by Scribner's in 1903, it went through many printings. A new edition with handsome photographs by J. Smeaton Chase appeared in 1918, another in 1930, with notes by the author's nephew, Dix Van Dyke, an authority on the Mojave Desert. John Van Dyke died in 1932, and the book eventually went out of print, although it was certainly not forgotten. In 1976, the Arizona Historical Society brought out a facsimile edition based on the edition of 1903, with an "Introduction" by Lawrence Clark Powell. That edition, followed so soon by this one, may well signal a wave of renewed interest in *The Desert*.

CONTENTS

THE DESERT

CHAPTER I

THE APPROACH

It is the last considerable group of mountains
between the divide and the low basin of the
Colorado desert. For days I have been watching them change color at sunset—watching the
canyons shift into great slashes of blue and
purple shadow, and the ridges flame with edgings of glittering fire. They are lonesome looking mountains lying off there by themselves on
the plain, so still, so barren, so blazing hot
under the sun. Forsaken of their kind, one
might not inappropriately call them the "Lost
Mountains"—the surviving remnant no doubt
of some noble range that long centuries ago
was beaten by wind and rain into desert sand.
And yet before one gets to them they may prove
quite formidable heights, with precipitous sides
and unsurmountable tops. Who knows ? Not
those with whom I am stopping, for they have

Desert
mountains.

1

not been there. They do not even know the name of them. The Papagoes leave them alone because there is no game in them. Evidently they are considered unimportant hills, nobody's hills, no man's range; but nevertheless I am off for them in the morning at daylight.

Unknown ranges.

I ride away through the thin mesquite and the little adobe ranch house is soon lost to view. The morning is still and perfectly clear. The stars have gone out, the moon is looking pale, the deep blue is warming, the sky is lightening with the coming day. How cool and crystalline the air! In a few hours the great plain will be almost like a fiery furnace under the rays of the summer sun, but now it is chilly. And in a few hours there will be rings and bands and scarves of heat set wavering across the waste upon the opalescent wings of the mirage; but now the air is so clear that one can see the breaks in the rocky face of the mountain range, though it is fully twenty miles away. It may be further. Who of the desert has not spent his day riding at a mountain and never even reaching its base? This is a land of illusions and thin air. The vision is so cleared at times that the truth itself is deceptive. But I shall ride on for several hours. If, by twelve

Early morning on the desert.

Air illusions.

o'clock, the foot hills are not reached, I shall turn back.

The summer heat has withered everything except the mesquite, the palo verde,* the grease wood, and the various cacti. Under foot there is a little dry grass, but more often patches of bare gravel and sand rolled in shallow beds that course toward the large valleys. *Sand forms in the valleys.* In the draws and flat places the fine sand lies thicker, is tossed in wave forms by the wind, and banked high against clumps of cholla or prickly pear. In the wash-outs and over the cut banks of the arroyos it is sometimes heaped in mounds and crests like driven snow. It blows here along the boundary line between Arizona and Sonora almost every day; and the tailing of the sands behind the bushes shows that the prevailing winds are from the Gulf region. A cool wind? Yes, but only by comparison with the north wind. When you feel it on your face you may think it the breath of some distant volcano. *Winds of the desert.*

How pale - blue the Lost Mountains look under the growing light. I am watching their edges develop into broken barriers of rock, and

* The use of Spanish names is compulsory. There are no English equivalents.

Sun shafts.

even as I watch the tallest tower of all is struck with a bright fawn color. It is the high point to catch the first shaft of the sun. Quickly the light spreads downward until the whole ridge is tinged by it, and the abrupt sides of porphyry begin to glow under it. It is not long before great shafts of light alternating with shadow stretch down the plain ahead of me. The sun is streaming through the tops of the eastern mountains and the sharp pointed pinnacles are cutting shadows in the broad beam of light.

The beauty of sunlight.

That beam of light! Was there ever anything so beautiful! How it flashes its color through shadow, how it gilds the tops of the mountains and gleams white on the dunes of the desert! In any land what is there more glorious than sunlight! Even here in the desert, where it falls fierce and hot as a rain of meteors, it is the one supreme beauty to which all things pay allegiance. The beast and the bird are not too fond of its heat and as soon as the sun is high in the heavens they seek cover in the canyons; but for all that the chief glory of the desert is its broad blaze of omnipresent light.

Yes, there is animal and bird life here though it is not always apparent unless you look for it.

Wrens and linnets are building nests in the cholla, and finches are singing from the top of the sahuaro.* There are plenty of reptiles, rabbits and ground squirrels quietly slipping out of your way; and now that the sun is up you can see a long sun-burned slant-of-hair trotting up yonder divide and casting an apprehensive head from side to side as he moves off. It is not often that the old gray wolf shows himself to the traveller. He is usually up in the mountains before sunrise. And seldom now does one see the desert antelope along the mesas, and yet off to the south you can see patches of white that come and go almost like flashing mirrors in the sun. They are stragglers from some band that have drifted up from central Sonora. No; they are not far away. A little mirage is already forming over that portion of the mesa and makes them look more distant than they are in reality. You can be deceived on the desert by the nearness of things quite as often as by their remoteness.

These desert mountains have a fashion of appearing distant until you are almost up to them. Then they seem to give up the game of deception and come out of their hiding-places. It is

Properly Saguaro.

Desert life.

Antelope.

The Lost Mountains.

just so with the mountains toward which I am riding. After several hours they seem to rise up suddenly in front of me and I am at their base. They are not high—perhaps fifteen hundred feet. The side near me is precipitous rock, weather-stained to a reddish-black. A ride around the bases discloses an almost complete perpendicular wall, slanting off half way down the sides into sloping beds of bowlders that have been shaken loose from the upper strata. A huge cleft in the western side—half barranca half canyon—seems to suggest a way to the summit.

Mountain walls.

The walking up the mountain is not the best in the world. It is over splintered rock, stepping from stone to stone, creeping along the backbone of bowlders, and worrying over rows of granite blocks. Presently the course seems to slip into a diagonal—a winding up and around the mountain—and ahead of me the stones begin to look peculiar, almost familiar. There seems to be a trail over the ledges and through the broken blocks; but what should make a trail up that deserted mountain? Mule-deer travelling toward the summit to lie down in the heat of the day? It is possible.

The ascent.

Deer trails. The track of a band of deer soon becomes a

beaten path, and animals are just as fond of a good path as humanity. By a strange coincidence at this very moment the sharp-toed print of a deer's hoof appears in the ground before me. But it looks a little odd. The impression is so clear cut that I stoop to examine it. It is with no little astonishment that I find it sunk in stone instead of earth—petrified in rock and overrun with silica. The bare suggestion gives one pause. How many thousands of years ago was that impression stamped upon the stone ? By what strange chance has it survived destruction ? And while it remains quite perfect to-day—the vagrant hoof-mark of a desert deer—what has become of the once carefully guarded footprints of the Sargons, the Pharaohs and the Cæsars ? With what contempt Nature sometimes plans the survival of the least fit, and breaks the conqueror on his shield !

Footprints.

Further up the mountain the deer-trail theory is abandoned—at least so far as recent times are concerned. The stones are worn too smooth, the larger ones have been pushed aside by something more intelligent than a mule-deer's hoof ; and in one place the trail seems to have been built up on the descending side. There is

The stone path.

not the slightest evidence, either by rub upon the rocks, or overturned stones, or scrape in the gravel, that any living thing has passed up this pathway for many years; and yet the trail is a distinct line of lighter colored stone stretch-

Following the trail.

ing ahead of me. It is a path worn in the rocks, and there is no grass or vine or weed to obliterate it. It leads on and up to the saddle of the mountain. There is a crevasse or chasm breaking through this saddle which might have been bridged at one time with mesquite trunks, but is now to be leaped if one would reach the summit. It is narrow only in one place and this is just where the trail happens to run. Across it, on the upper side, there is a horse-

Defensive walls.

shoe shaped enclosure of stone. It is only a few feet in diameter, and the upper layers of stone have fallen; but the little wall still stands as high as one's waist. Could this have been a sentinel box used to guard the passage of the trail at this place?

Higher and still higher until at last the mountain broadens into a flat top. I am so eager to gain the height and am expecting so much that at first I overlook what is before me.

The summit.

Gradually I make out a long parapet of loose stone on the trail side of the mountain which joins on to steep cliffs on the other sides. A conclusion is instantly jumped at, for the imagination will not make haste slowly under such circumstances. These are the ruins of a once fortified camp.

I wander about the flat top of the mountain and slowly there grows into recognizable form a great rectangle enclosed by large stones placed about two feet apart. There is no doubt about the square and in one corner of it there seems an elevated mound covered with high-piled *The fortified camp.* stones that would indicate a place for burials. But not a trace of pottery or arrow-heads ; and about the stones only faint signs of fire which might have come from volcanic action as readily as from domestic hearths. Upon the side of one of the large rocks are some characters in red ochre ; and on the ground near a pot-hole in the rock, something that the imagination might torture into a rude pestle for grinding maize.

The traces of human activity are slight. Nature has been wearing them away and reclaiming her own on the mountain top. Grease *Nature's reclamations.* wood is growing where once a floor was beaten hard as iron by human feet ; out of the burial mound rises a giant sahuaro whose branching

arms give the look of the cross; and beside
the sahuaro rests a tall yucca with four feet of
clustering bellflowers swinging from its top.

Mountain dwellers.

And who were they who built these stone walls,
these primitive entrenchments? When and
where did they come from and what brought
them here? The hands that executed this
rough work were certainly untrained. Indians?
Very likely. Perhaps some small band that had
taken up a natural defence in the mountains
because too feeble in numbers to fight in the
open. Here from this lookout they could watch
the country for a hundred miles around. Here
the scouts could see far away the thin string of
foemen winding snake-like over the ridges of
the desert, could see them grow in size and
count their numbers, could look down upon
them at the foot of the mountain and yell back
defiance to the challenge coming up the steep

Invading hosts.

sides. Brave indeed the invaders that would
pluck the eagles from that eerie nest! Climbing a hill against a shower of arrows, spears,
and bowlders is to fight at a terrible disad-
vantage.

Starve them out? Yes; but the ones at the
bottom would starve as quickly as those at the
top. Cut off their water supply? Yes; but

where did either besieged or besieger get water? *Water and food supplies.*
If there was ever a spring in the mountain it
long ago dried up, for there is no trace of it to-
day. Possibly the mountain-dwellers knew of
some arroyo where by digging in the sand they
could get water. And possibly they carried
it in ollas up the stone trail to their mountain
home where they stored it in the rocks against
the wrath of a siege to come. No doubt they
took thought for trouble, and being native to
the desert they could stand privation better
than their enemies.

How long ago did that aboriginal band come *The aborigines.*
trailing over these trackless deserts to find and
make a home in a barren mountain standing
in a bed of sand ? Who can tell ? A geologist
might make the remains of their fort an illustration of the Stone Age and talk of unknown centuries ; an iconoclast might claim
that it was merely a Mexican corral built to
hide stolen horses ; but a plain person of the
southwest would say that it was an old Indian
camp. The builders of the fortification and the
rectangle worked with stone because there was
no other material. The man of the Stone Age
exists to-day contemporary with civilized man.
Possibly he always did. And it may be that

Historic periods.

some day Science will conclude that historic periods do not invariably happen, that there is not always a sequential evolution, and that the white race does not necessarily require a flat-headed mass of stupidity for an ancestor.

But what brought them to seek a dwelling place in the desert ? Were they driven out from the more fertile tracts ? Perhaps. Did they find this a country where game was plentiful and the conditions of life comparatively easy ? It is possible. Or was it that they loved the

The open desert.

open country, the hot sun, the treeless wastes, the great stretches of mesa, plain and valley ? Ah ; that is more than likely. Mankind has always loved the open plains. He is like an antelope and wishes to see about him in all directions. Perhaps, too, he was born with a pre-dilection for "the view," but that is no easy matter to prove. It is sometimes assumed that humanity had naturally a sense and a feeling for the beautiful because the primitives deco-rated pottery and carved war-clubs and totem-posts. Again perhaps ; but from war-clubs and totem-posts to sunsets and mountain shadows

Perception of beauty.

—the love of the beautiful in nature—is a very long hark. The peons and Indians in Sonora cannot see the pinks and purples in the moun-

tain shadows at sunset. They are astonished at
your question for they see nothing but mountains. And you may vainly exhaust ingenuity
trying to make a Pagago see the silvery sheen
of the mesquite when the low sun is streaming
across its tops. He sees only mesquite—the
same dull mesquite through which he has
chased rabbits from infancy.

No ; it is not likely that the tribe ever chose
this abiding place for its scenery. A sensitive *Sense of beauty.*
feeling for sound, or form, or color, an impres-
sionable nervous organization, do not belong to
the man with the hoe, much less to the man
with the bow. It is to be feared that they are
indicative of some physical degeneration, some
decline in bone and muscle, some abnormal
development of the emotional nature. They
travel side by side with high civilization and
are the premonitory symptoms of racial decay.
But are we correct in assuming that because
the red man does not see a colored shadow
therefore he is blind to every charm and sublimity of nature ?

These mountain-dwellers, always looking out
from their height, must have seen and re- *Mountain "view."*
marked the large features of the desert—the
great masses of form, the broad blocks of color.

They knew the long undulations of the valley-plain were covered with sharp, broken rock, but from this height surely they must have noticed how soft as velvet they looked, how smoothly they rolled from one into another, how perfectly they curved, how symmetrically they waved. And the long lines of the divides, lessening to the west—their ridges of grease wood showing a peculiar green like the crests of sea-waves in storm—did they not see them ? Did they not look down on the low neighboring hills and

The desert colors.

know that they were pink, terra-cotta, orange-colored—all the strange hues that may be compounded of clay and mineral—with here and there a crowning mass of white quartz or a far-extending outcrop of shale stained blue and green with copper ? Doubtless, a wealth of color and atmospheric effect was wasted upon the aboriginal retina ; but did it not take note of the deep orange sunsets, the golden fringed heaps of cumulus, and the tongues of fire that curled from every little cirrus cloud that lingered in the western sky ?

And how often they must have looked out

Looking down to the desert.

and down to the great basin of the desert where cloud and sky, mountain and mesa, seemed to dissolve into a pink mist ! It was not an unknown land to them and yet it had its terrors. Tradition told that the Evil Spirit dwelt there, and it was his hot breath that came up every morning on the wind, scorching and burning the brown faces of the mountain-dwellers! Fire!—he dwelt in fire. Whence came all the fierce glow of sunset down over that desert if it was not the reflection from his dwelling place? The very mountain peaks flared red at times, and in the old days there were rivers of fire. The petrified waves and eddies of those rivers were still visible in the lava streams. Were there not also great flames beneath the sands that threw up hot water and boiled great volcanoes of mud? And along the base of many a cliff were there not jets of steam and smoke blown out from the heart of the mountains?

The land of fire.

It was a land of fire. No food, no grass, no water. There were places in the canyons where occasionally a little stream was found forcing itself up through the rock; but frequently it was salt or, worse yet, poisoned with copper or arsenic. How often the tribe had lost from its numbers—slain by the heat and drought in that waste! More than once the bodies had been found by crossing bands and always the same tale was told. The victims were half

Drought and heat.

buried in sand, not decayed, but withered like the grass on the lomas.

Mystery—a mystery as luminous and yet as impenetrable as its own mirage—seemed always hanging over that low-lying waste. It was a vast pit dug under the mountain bases. The mountains themselves were bare crags of fire in the sunlight, and the sands of the pit grew only cactus and grease wood. There were tracts where nothing at all grew—miles upon miles of absolute waste with the pony's feet breaking through an alkaline crust. And again, there were dry lakes covered with silt ; and vast beds of sand and gypsum, white as snow and fine as dust. The pony's feet plunged in and came out leaving no trail. The surface smoothed over as though it were water. Fifty miles away one could see the desert sand-whirls moving slowly over the beds in tall columns two thousand feet high and shining like shafts of marble in the sunlight. How majestically they moved, their feet upon earth, their heads towering into the sky !

And then the desert winds that raised at times such furious clouds of sand ! All the air shone like gold dust and the sun turned red as blood. Ah ! what a stifling sulphureous

Desert mystery.

Sand and gypsum.

Sand-whirls.

air! Even on the mountain tops that heavy air could be felt, and down in the desert itself the driving particles of sand cut the face and hands like blizzard-snow. The ponies could not be made to face it. They turned their backs to the wind and hung their heads between their fore feet. And how that wind roared and whistled through the thin grease wood! The scrubby growths leaned and bent in the blast, the sand piled high on the trunks; and nothing but the enormous tap-roots kept them from being wrenched from the earth.

Desert storms.

And danger always followed the high winds. They blew the sands in clouds that drifted full and destroyed the trails. In a single night they would cover up a water hole, and in a few days fill in an arroyo where water could be got by digging. The sands drove like breakers on a beach, washing and wearing everything up to the bases of the mountains. And the fine sand reached still higher. It whirled up the canyons and across the saddles, it eddied around the enormous taluses, it even flung itself upon the face walls of the mountain and left the smoothing marks of its fingers upon the sharp pinnacles of the peak.

Drift of sand.

It was in winter when the winds were fiercest.

Winter cold. With them at times came a sharp cold, the
more biting for the thin dry air of the desert.
All the warmth seemed blown out of the basin
with a breath, and its place filled by a storm-
wind from the north that sent the condor
wheeling down the blast and made the coyote
shiver on the hill. How was it possible that
such a furnace could grow so cold ! And once
or more each winter, when the sky darkened
with clouds, there was a fall of snow that for
an hour or so whitened the desert mountains
and then passed away. At those times the
springs were frozen, the high sierras were
Snow on snow-bound, and down in the desert it seemed
desert. as though a great frost-sheet had been let down
from above. The brown skins for all their
deer-hide clothing were red with cold, and the
breath blown from the pony's nostrils was
white as smoke.

A waste of intense heat and cold, of drouth
and cloud-bursts, of winds and lightning, of
storm and death, what could make any race of
hunters or band of red men care for it ? What
was the attraction, wherein the fascination ?
Sea and How often have we wondered why the sailor
sand. loves the sea, why the Bedouin loves the sand !
What is there but a strip of sky and another

strip of sand or water ? But there is a simplicity about large masses — simplicity in
breadth, space and distance—that is inviting
and ennobling. And there is something very
restful about the horizontal line. Things that
lie flat are at peace and the mind grows peace-
ful with them. Furthermore, the waste places
of the earth, the barren deserts, the tracts forsaken of men and given over to loneliness, have
a peculiar attraction of their own. The weird
solitude, the great silence, the grim desolation,
are the very things with which every desert
wanderer eventually falls in love. You think
that very strange perhaps ? Well, the beauty
of the ugly was sometime a paradox, but to-day
people admit its truth ; and the grandeur of
the desolate is just as paradoxical, yet the
desert gives it proof.

*Grim des-
olation.*

But the sun-tanned people who lived on this
mountain top never gave thought to masses,
or horizontal lines, or paradoxes. They lived
here, it may be from necessity at first, and then
stayed on because they loved the open wind-
blown country, the shining orange-hued sands,
the sweeping mesas, the great swing of the
horizontal circle, the flat desolation, the unbroken solitude. Nor ever knew why they

*Love for
the desert.*

loved it. They were content and that was
enough.

What finally became of them ? Who knows ?
One by one they passed away, or perhaps were
all slaughtered in a night by the fierce band
newly come to numbers called the Apaches.
This stone wall stands as their monument, but
The descent. it tells no date or tale of death. As I descend
the trail of stone the fancy keeps harping on
the countless times the bare feet must have
rubbed those blocks of syenite and porphyry
to wear them so smooth. Have there been no
others to clamber up these stairs of stone ?
What of the Padres — were they not here ?
As I ride off across the plain to the east the
thought is of the heroism, the self-abnega-
tion, the undying faith of those followers of
Loyola and Xavier who came into this waste so
many years ago. How idle seem all the specious
The Padres. tales of Jesuitism and priestcraft. The Padres
were men of soul, unshrinking faith, and a perseverance almost unparalleled in the annals of
history. The accomplishments of Columbus,
of Cortez, of Coronado were great ; but what
of those who first ventured out upon these sands
and erected missions almost in the heart of the
desert, who single-handed coped with dangers

from man and nature, and who lived and died
without the slightest hope of reward here on
earth ? Has not the sign of the cross cast more
men in heroic mould than ever the glitter of
the crown or the flash of the sword ?

And thinking such thoughts I turn to take a
final view of the mountain ; and there on the
fortified top something rears itself against the
sky like the cross-hilt of a sword. It is the
giant sahuaro with its rising arms, and beside
it the cream-white bloom of the yucca shining
in the sunlight seems like a lamp illuminating
it. The good Padres have gone and their mis-
sion churches are crumbling back to the earth
from which they were made ; but the light of *Light of the cross.*
the cross still shines along the borders of this
desert land. The flame, that through them the
Spirit kindled, still burns ; and in every Indian
village, in every Mexican adobe, you will see on
the wall the wooden or grass-woven cross. On
the high hills and at the cross-roads it stands,
roughly hewn from mesquite and planted in a
cone of stones. It is now always weather-stained
and sun-cracked, but still the sign before which
the peon and the Indian bow the head and whis-
per words of prayer. The dwellers beside the *Aboriginal faith.*
desert have cherished what the inhabitants of

the fertile plains have thrown away. They and
their forefathers have never known civilization,
and never suffered from the blight of doubt.
Of a simple nature, they have lived in a simple
way, close to their mother earth, beside the
desert they loved, and (let us believe it !) nearer
to the God they worshipped.

CHAPTER II

THE MAKE OF THE DESERT

THE first going - down into the desert is always something of a surprise. The fancy has pictured one thing; the reality shows quite another thing. Where and how did we gain the idea that the desert was merely a sea of sand? Did it come from that geography of our youth with the illustration of the sand-storm, the flying camel, and the over-excited Bedouin? Or have we been reading strange tales told by travellers of perfervid imagination—the Marco Polos of to-day? There is, to be sure, some modicum of truth even in the statement that misleads. There are " seas " or lakes or ponds of sand on every desert; but they are not so vast, not so oceanic, that you ever lose sight of the land.

Sea of sand.

What land? Why, the mountains. The desert is traversed by many mountain ranges, some of them long, some short, some low, and some rising upward ten thousand feet. They

Mountain ranges on the desert.

23

are always circling you with a ragged horizon, dark-hued, bare-faced, barren—just as truly desert as the sands which were washed down from them. Between the ranges there are wide-expanding plains or valleys. The most arid portions of the desert lie in the basins of these great valleys—flat spaces that were once the beds of lakes, but are now dried out and left perhaps with an alkaline deposit that prevents vegetation. Through these valleys run arroyos or dry stream-beds—shallow channels where gravel and rocks are rolled during cloudbursts and where sands drift with every wind. At times the valleys are more diversified, that is, broken by benches of land called mesas, dotted with small groups of hills called lomas, crossed by long stratified faces of rock called escarpments.

Plains, valleys, and mesas.

With these large features of landscape common to all countries, how does the desert differ from any other land ? Only in the matter of water—the lack of it. If Southern France should receive no more than two inches of rain a year for twenty years it would, at the end of that time, look very like the Sahara, and the flashing Rhone would resemble the sluggish yellow Nile. If the Adirondack region in New

Effect of drought.

York were comparatively rainless for the same length of time we should have something like the Mojave Desert, with the Hudson changed into the red Colorado. The conformations of the lands are not widely different, but their surface appearances are as unlike as it is possible to imagine.

For the whole face of a land is changed by the rains. With them come meadow-grasses *The effect of rains.* and flowers, hillside vines and bushes, fields of yellow grain, orchards of pink-white blossoms. Along the mountain sides they grow the forests of blue-green pine, on the peaks they put white caps of snow ; and in the valleys they gather their waste waters into shining rivers and flashing lakes. This is the very sheen and sparkle —the witchery—of landscape which lend allurement to such countries as New England, France, or Austria, and make them livable and lovable lands.

But the desert has none of these charms. *Harshness of the desert.* Nor is it a livable place. There is not a thing about it that is "pretty," and not a spot upon it that is "picturesque" in any Berkshire-Valley sense. The shadows of foliage, the drift of clouds, the fall of rain upon leaves, the sound of running waters—all the gentler qualities of

nature that minor poets love to juggle with—
are missing on the desert. It is stern, harsh,
and at first repellent. But what tongue shall
tell the majesty of it, the eternal strength of it,
the poetry of its wide-spread chaos, the sublimity of its lonely desolation! And who shall
paint the splendor of its light; and from the
rising up of the sun to the going down of the
moon over the iron mountains, the glory of its
A gaunt land. wondrous coloring! It is a gaunt land of
splintered peaks, torn valleys, and hot skies.
And at every step there is the suggestion of the
fierce, the defiant, the defensive. Everything
within its borders seems fighting to maintain
itself against destroying forces. There is a war
of elements and a struggle for existence going
on here that for ferocity is unparalleled elsewhere in nature.

Conditions of life. The feeling of fierceness grows upon you as
you come to know the desert better. The sun-
shafts are falling in a burning shower upon
rock and dune, the winds blowing with the
breath of far-off fires are withering the bushes
and the grasses, the sands drifting higher and
higher are burying the trees and reaching up as
though they would overwhelm the mountains,
the cloud-bursts are rushing down the moun-

tain's side and through the torn arroyos as though they would wash the earth into the sea. The life, too, on the desert is peculiarly savage. *The incessant struggle.* It is a show of teeth in bush and beast and reptile. At every turn one feels the presence of the barb and thorn, the jaw and paw, the beak and talon, the sting and the poison thereof. Even the harmless Gila monster flattens his body on a rock and hisses a "Don't step on me." There is no living in concord or brotherhood here. Everything is at war with its neighbor, and the conflict is unceasing.

Yet this conflict is not so obvious on the face of things. You hear no clash or crash or snarl. *Elemental warfare.* The desert is overwhelmingly silent. There is not a sound to be heard; and not a thing moves save the wind and the sands. But you look up at the worn peaks and the jagged barrancas, you look down at the wash-outs and piled bowlders, you look about at the wind-tossed, half-starved bushes; and, for all the silence, you know that there is a struggle for life, a war for place, going on day by day.

How is it possible under such conditions for much vegetation to flourish ? The grasses are *Desert vegetation.* scanty, the grease wood and cactus grow in patches, the mesquite crops out only along the

dry river-beds. All told there is hardly enough
covering to hide the anatomy of the earth.
And the winds are always blowing it aside.
You have noticed how bare and bony the hills
of New England are in winter when the trees
are leafless and the grasses are dead ? You have
seen the rocks loom up harsh and sharp, the
ledges assume angles, and the backbone and ribs
of the open field crop out of the soil ? The
desert is not unlike that all the year round.
To be sure there are snow-like driftings of sand
that muffle certain edges. Valleys, hills, and
even mountains are turned into rounded lines
by it at times. But the drift rolled high in
one place was cut out from some other place ;
and always there are *vertebræ* showing—elbows

*Protruding
edges.*

and shoulders protruding through the yellow
byssus of sand.

The shifting sands ! Slowly they move, wave

*Shifting
sands.*

upon wave, drift upon drift ; but by day and
by night they gather, gather, gather. They
overwhelm, they bury, they destroy, and then
a spirit of restlessness seizes them and they
move off elsewhere, swirl upon swirl, line upon
line, in serpentine windings that enfold some
new growth or fill in some new valley in the
waste. So it happens that the surface of the

desert is far from being a permanent affair. There is hardly enough vegetation to hold the sands in place. With little or no restraint upon them they are transported hither and yon at the mercy of the winds.

Yet the desert winds hardly blow where they list. They follow certain channels or "draws" through the mountain ranges; and the reason for their doing so is plain enough. During the day the intense heat of the desert, meeting with only a thin dry air above it, rises rapidly skyward leaving a vast vacuum below that must be filled with a colder air from without. This colder air on the southern portion of the Colorado Desert comes in from the Gulf region. One can feel it in the passes of the mountains about Baboquivari, rushing up toward the heated portions of Arizona around Tucson. And the hotter the day the stronger the inward rush of the wind. Some days it will blow at the rate of fifty miles an hour until sunset, and then with a cessation of radiation the wind stops and the night is still.

Desert winds.

Radiation of heat.

On the western portions of the Colorado the wind comes from the Pacific across Southern California. The hot air from the desert goes up and out over the Coast Range, reaching sea-

ward. How far out it goes is unknown, but
when it has cooled off it descends and flows
back toward the land as the daily sea-breeze.
It re-enters the desert through such loop holes
Prevailing in the Coast Range as the San Gorgonio Pass—
winds. the old Puerta de San Carlos—above Indio.
The rush of it through that pass is quite violent at times. For wind is very much like
water and seeks the least obstructed way. Its
goal is usually the hottest and the lowest place
on the desert—such a place, for example, as
Salton, though I am not prepared to point out
the exact spot on the desert that the winds
choose as a target. On the Mojave Desert at
the north their action is similar, though there
they draw down from the Mount Whitney region as well as from the Pacific.

In open places these desert winds are sometimes terrific in force though usually they are
moderate and blow with steadiness from certain
directions. As you feel them softly blowing
Wear of against your cheek it is hard to imagine that they
the winds. have any sharp edge to them. Yet about you
on every side is abundant evidence of their
works. The sculptor's sand-blast works swifter
but not surer. Granite and porphyry cannot
withstand them, and in time they even cut

through the glassy surface of lava. Their wear
is not here nor there, but all over, everywhere.
The edge of the wind is always against the stone.
Continually there is the slow erosion of canyon,
crag, and peak; forever there is a gnawing at
the bases and along the face-walls of the great
sierras. Grain by grain, the vast foundations,
the beetling escarpments, the high domes in air
are crumbled away and drifted into the valleys. *Erosion of mountains.*
Nature heaved up these mountains at one time
to fulfil a purpose : she is now taking them
down to fulfil another purpose. If she has
not water to work with here as elsewhere she is
not baffled of her purpose. Wind and sand answer quite as well.

But the cutting of the wind is not always
even or uniform, owing to the inequalities in
the fibre of rock ; and often odd effects are produced by the softer pieces of rock wearing away
first and leaving the harder section exposed to
view. Frequently these remainders take on
fantastic shapes and are likened to things human, such as faces, heads, and hands. In the
San Gorgonio Pass the rock-cuttings are in *Rock-cutting.*
parallel lines, and occasionally a row of gar-
nets in the rock will make the jewel-pointed
fingers of a hand protruding from the parent

body.* Again shafts of hard granite may make tall spires and turrets upon a mountain peak, a vein of quartz may bulge out in a white or yellow or rose-colored band ; and a ridge of black lava, reaching down the side of a foot-hill, may creep and heave like the backbone of an enormous dragon.

Fantastic forms.

Perhaps the greatest erosion is in the passes through which the winds rush into the desert. Here they not only eat into the ledges and cut away the rock faces, but they make great washouts in the desert itself. These trenches look in every respect as though caused by water. In fact the effects of wind and water are often so inextricably mixed that not even an expert geologist would be able to say where the one leaves off and the other begins. The shallow caves of the mountains—too high up for any wave action from sea or lake, and too deep to be reached by rains—have all the rounded appearance of water-worn receptacles. One can almost see the water-lines upon the walls. But the sand-heaped floor suggests that the agent of erosion was the wind.

Wash-outs.

Sand-lines in caves.

Yes ; there is some water on the deserts, some

---

* Professor Blake of the University of Arizona has called my attention to this.

rainfall each year. Even Sahara gets its occasional showers, and the Colorado and the Mo-
jave show many traces of the cloud-burst. The *Cloud-bursts.*
dark thunder-clouds that occasionally gather
over the desert seem at times to reserve all their
stores of rain for one place. The fall is usually
short-lived but violent ; and its greatest force
is always on the mountains. There is no sod,
no moss, to check or retard the flood ; and the
result is a great rush of water to the low places.
In the canyons the swollen streams roll down *Canyon streams.*
bowlders that weigh tons, and in the ravines
many a huge barranca is formed in a single
hour by these rushing waters. On the lomas
and sloping valleys they are not less destructive,
running in swift streams down the hollows, and
whirling stones, sand, and torn bushes into the
old river-beds.

In a very short time there is a great torrent
pouring down the valley—a torrent composed
of water, sand, and gravel in about equal parts.
It is a yellow, thick stream that has nothing but
disaster for the man or beast that seeks to swim *Desert floods.*
it. Many a life has been lost there. The great
onset of the water destroys anything like buoy-
ancy, and the tendency is to drag down and
roll the swimmer like a bowlder. Even the

enormous strength of the grizzly bear has been
known to fail him in these desert rivers. They
boil and seethe as though they were hot; and
they rush on against banks, ripping out the

Power of water. long roots of mesquite, and swirling away tons
of undermined gravel as though it were only so
much snow. At last after miles of this mill-
racing the force begins to diminish, the streams
reach the flat lake-beds and spread into broad,
thin sheets; and soon they have totally vanished, leaving scarce a rack behind.

The desert rainfall comes quickly and goes
quickly. The sands drink it up, and it sinks
to the rock strata, where, following the ledges, it
is finally shelved into some gravel-bed. There,
perhaps a hundred feet under the sand, it slow-

Water-pockets. ly oozes away to the river or the Gulf. There
is none of it remains upon the surface except
perhaps a pool caught in a clay basin, or a
catch of water in a rocky bowl of some canyon.
Occasionally one meets with a little stream
where a fissure in the rock and a pressure from
below forces up some of the water; but these

No running streams. springs are of very rare occurrence. And they
always seem a little strange. A brook that ran
on the top of the ground would be an anomaly
here; and after one lives many months on the

desert and returns to a well-watered country, the last thing he becomes accustomed to is the sight of running water.

In every desert there are isolated places where water stands in pools, fed by underground springs, where mesquite and palms grow, and where there is a show of coarse grass over some acres. These are the so-called oases in the waste that travellers have pictured *Oases in the* as Gardens of Paradise, and poets have used *waste.* for centuries as illustrations of happiness surrounded by despair. To tell the truth they are wretched little mud-holes; and yet because of their few trees and their pockets of yellow brackish water they have an appearance of unreality. They are strange because bright-green foliage and moisture of any kind seem out of place on the desert.

Yet surely there was plenty of water here at one time. Everywhere you meet with the dry lake-bed—its flat surface devoid of life and often glimmering white with salt. These beds are no doubt of recent origin geologically, and were never more than the catch-basins of sur- *Catch-* face water; but long before ever they were *basins.* brought forth the whole area of the desert was under the sea. To-day one may find on

the high table-lands sea-shells in abundance.
The petrified clams are precisely like the live
clams that one picks up on the western coast
of Mexico. The corals, barnacles, dried sponge
forms, and cellular rocks do not differ from
those in the Gulf of California. The change
Old sea-
beds.
from sea to shore, and from shore to table-land
and mountain, no doubt took place very slowly. Just how many centuries ago who shall
say ? Geologists may guess and laymen may
doubt, but the Keeper of the Seals says nothing.

Nor is it known just when the porphyry
mountains were roasted to a dark wine-red,
and the foot-hills burnt to a terra-cotta orange.
Fire has been at work here as well as wind
Volcanic
action.
and water. The whole country has a burnt
and scorched look proceeding from something
more fiery than sunlight. Volcanoes have left
their traces everywhere. You can still see the
streams of lava that have chilled as they ran.
The blackened cones with their craters exist ;
and about them, for many miles, there are
Lava
streams.
great lakes and streams of reddish-black lava,
frozen in swirls and pools, cracked like glass,
broken into blocks like a ruined pavement.
Wherever you go on the desert you meet with

chips and breaks of lava, showing that at one time there must have been quantities of it belched out of the volcanoes.

There were convulsions in those days when the sea washed close to the bases of the mountains. Through the crevasses and fissures in the rocks the water crept into the fires of the earth, and explosions—volcanic eruptions—were the result. Wandering over these stony tracks you might fancy that all strata and all geological *Geological ages.* ages were blown into discord by those explosions. For here are many kinds of splintered and twisted rocks—rocks aqueous and igneous, gritstones, conglomerates, shales, slates, syenite, basalt. And everywhere the white coatings of carbonate of lime that look as though they were run hot from a puddling furnace ; and the dust of sulphur, copper, and *Kinds of rock.* iron blown upon granite as though oxidized by fire.

The evidence for glaciers is not so convincing. There is no apparent sign of an ice age. *Glaciers.* Occasionally one sees scratches upon mountain walls that are suspicious, or heaps of sand and gravel that look as though pushed into the small valleys by some huge force. And again there are places on the Mojave where windrows of heavy bowlders are piled on either side of mountain water-courses, looking as though ice may have caused their peculiar placing. But *Land slips.* there is no certainty about any of these. Land slips may have made the windrows as easily as ice slips ; and water can heap mounds of sand and gravel as readily as glaciers. One cannot trace the geological ages with such facility. Things sometimes "just happen," in spite of scientific theories.

Movement of stones. Besides, the movement of the stones into the valleys is going on continuously, irrespective of glaciers. They are first broken from the peaks by erosion, and then they fall into what is called *The talus.* a talus—a great slope of stone blocks beginning half way down the mountain and often reaching to the base or foot. Many of them, of course, are rolled over steep declivities into the canyons and thence carried down by flood waters ; but the talus is the more uniform method for bowlders reaching the plain.

In the first stage of the talus the blocks are ragged-edged and as large as a barrel. Nothing whatever grows upon the slope. It is as bare as the side of a volcanic crater. And just as difficult to walk over. The talus is added to at the top by the falling rock of the face-wall, and it

is losing at the bottom by the under blocks
grinding away to stone and gravel. The flattening out at the bottom, the breaking up of
the blocks, and the push-out of the mountain
foot upon the plain is the second stage of the
talus. In almost all the large valleys of the
desert the depressed talus extends, sometimes
miles in length, out from the foot of the moun-
tain range. When it finally slips down into the *Stages of the talus.*
valley and becomes a flat floor it has entered
upon its third and last stage. It is then the
ordinary valley-bed covered with its cactus and
cut by its arroyos. Yet this valley-floor instead
of being just one thing is really many things—
or rather made up of many different materials
and showing many different surfaces.

You may spend days and weeks studying the
make-up of these desert-floors. Beyond Yuma *Desert-floors.*
on the Colorado there are thousands of acres of
mosaic pavement, made from tiny blocks of
jasper, carnelian, agate—a pavement of pebbles
so hard that a horse's hoof will make no impression upon it—wind-swept, clean, compact
as though pressed down by a roller. One can
imagine it made by the winds that have cut
and drifted away the light sands and allowed
the pebbles to settle close together until they

have become wedged in a solid surface. For no known reason other portions of the desert are

Sandstone blocks.

covered with blocks of red-incrusted sandstone —the incrustation being only above the sand-line. In the lake-beds there is usually a surface of fine silt. It is not a hard surface though it often has a crust upon it that a wildcat can walk upon, but a horse or a man would pound through as easily as through crusted snow.

Salt-beds.

The salt-beds are of sporadic appearance and hardly count as normal features of the desert. They are often quite beautiful in appearance. The one on the Colorado near Salton is hard as ice, white, and after sunset it often turns blue, yellow, or crimson, dependent upon the sky overhead which it reflects. Borax and gypsum-beds are even scarcer than the salt-beds. They are also white and often very brilliant reflectors

Sand-beds.

of the sky. The sand-beds are, of course, more frequently met with than any others; and yet your horse does not go knee-deep in sand for any great distance. It is too light, and is drifted too easily by the winds. Bowlders, gravel, and general mountain wash is the most common flooring of all.

The mountains whence all the wash comes, are mere ranges of rock. In the canyons, where there is perhaps some underground water, there are occasionally found trees and large bushes, and the very high sierras have forests of pine belted about their tops; but usually the desert ranges are barren. They never bore fruit. The washings from them are grit and fry of rock but no vegetable mould. The black dirt that lies a foot or more in depth upon the surface of the eastern prairies, showing the many years accumulations of decayed grasses and weeds, is not known anywhere on the desert. The slight vegetation that grows never has a chance to turn into mould. And besides, nothing ever rots or decays in these sands. Iron will not rust, nor tin tarnish, nor flesh mortify. The grass and the shrub wither and are finally cut into pieces by flying sands. Sometimes you may see small particles of grass or twigs heaped about an ant-hill, or find them a part of a bird's nest in a cholla; but usually they turn to dry dust and blow with the wind—at the wind's will.

Mountain vegetation.

Withered grasses.

The desert mountains gathered in clusters along the waste, how old and wrinkled, how set and determined they look! Somehow they remind you of a clinched hand with the knuckles turned skyward. They have strength and bulk, the suggestion of quiescent force.

*Barren
rock.*
Barren rock and nothing more ; but what could
better epitomize power ! The heave of the
enormous ridge, the loom of the domed top,
the bulk and body of the whole are colossal.
Rising as they do from flat sands they give the
impression of things deep-based—veritable islands of porphyry bent upward from a yellow
*Mountain
colors.*
sea. They are so weather-stained, so worn,
that they are not bright in coloring. Usually
they assume a dull garnet-red, or the red of
peroxide of iron ; but occasionally at sunset
they warm in color and look fire-red through
the pink haze.

The more abrupt ranges that appear younger
*Saw-toothed
ridges.*
because of their saw-toothed ridges and broken
peaks, are often much finer in coloring. They
have needles that are lifted skyward like Moslem minarets or cathedral spires ; and at evening, if there is a yellow light, they shine like
brazen spear-points set against the sky. It is
astonishing that dull rock can disclose such
marvellous coloring. The coloring is not local
in the rock, nor yet again entirely reflected.
Desert atmosphere, with which we shall have to
reckon hereafter, has much to do with it.

And whether at sunset, at sunrise, or at midnight, how like watch-towers these mountains

stand above the waste! One can almost fancy that behind each dome and rampart there are cloud-like Genii—spirits of the desert—keeping guard over this kingdom of the sun. And what a far-reaching kingdom they watch! Plain upon plain leads up and out to the horizon—far as the eye can see—in undulations of gray and gold; ridge upon ridge melts into the blue of the distant sky in lines of lilac and purple; fold upon fold over the mesas the hot air drops its veilings of opal and topaz. Yes; it is the kingdom of sun-fire. For every color in the scale is attuned to the key of flame, every air-wave comes with the breath of flame, every sunbeam falls as a shaft of flame. There is no questioning who is sovereign in these dominions.

Seen from the peaks.

Sun-fire kingdom.

CHAPTER III

THE BOTTOM OF THE BOWL

Early geological days.

In the ancient days when the shore of the Pacific was young, when the white sierras had only recently been heaved upward and the desert itself was in a formative stage, the ocean reached much farther inland than at the present time. It pushed through many a pass and flooded many a depression in the sands, as its wave-marks upon granite bases and its numerous beaches still bear witness. In those days that portion of the Colorado Desert known as the Salton Basin did not exist. The Gulf of California extended as far north as the San Bernardino Range and as far west as the Pass of San Gorgonio. Its waters stood deep where now lies the road-bed of the Southern Pacific railway, and all the country from Indio almost to the Colorado River was a blue sea. The Bowl was full. No one knew if it had a bottom or imagined that it would ever be emptied of water and given over to the drifting sands.

The former Gulf.

44

No doubt the tenure of the sea in this Salton Basin was of long duration. The sand-dunes still standing along the northern shore—fifty feet high and shining like hills of chalk—were not made in a month ; nor was the long shelving beach beneath them — still covered with sea-shells and pebbles and looking as though washed by the waves only yesterday—formed in a day. Both dunes and beach are plainly visible winding across the desert for many miles. The southwestern shore, stretching under a spur of the Coast Range, shows the same formation in its beach - line. The old bays and lagoons that led inland from the sea, the river-beds that brought down the surface waters from the mountains, the inlets and natural harbors are all in place. Some of them are drifted half full of sand, but they have not lost their identity. And out in the sea-bed still stand masses of cellular rock, honeycombed and water-worn (and now for many years wind-worn), showing the places where once rose the reefs of the ancient sea.

Sea-beaches on desert.

Harbors and reefs.

These are the only records that tell of the sea's occupation. The Indians have no tradition about it. Yet when the sea was there the Indian tribes were there also. Along the bases of the San Bernardino and San Jacinto Ranges there are indications of cave-dwelling, *Indian remains.* rock-built squares that doubtless were fortified camps, heaps of stone that might have been burial-mounds. Everywhere along the ancient shores and beaches you pick up pieces of pottery, broken ollas, stone pestels and mortars, axe - heads, obsidian arrow - heads, flint spearpoints, agate beads. There is not the slightest doubt that the shores were inhabited. It was a warm nook, accessible to the mountains and the Pacific; in fact, just the place where tribes would naturally gather. Branches of *The Cocopas.* the Yuma Indians, like the Cocopas, overran all this country when the Padres first crossed the desert; and it was probably their forefathers who lived by the shores of this Upper Gulf. No doubt they were fishermen, traders and fighters, like their modern representatives on Tiburon Island; and no doubt they fished and fought and were happy by the shores of the mountain-locked sea.

But there came a time when there was a disturbance of the existing conditions in the Up- *The Colorado River.* per Gulf. Century after century the Colorado River had been carrying down to the sea its burden of sedimental sand and silt. It had been entering the Gulf far down on the eastern side at an acute angle. Gradually its deposits had been building up, banking up ; and gradually the river had been pushing them out and across the Gulf in a southwesterly direction. Finally there was formed a delta dam stretching from shore to shore. The tides no longer brought water up and around the bases of the big mountains. Communication with the sea was cut off and what was once the top of the Gulf changed into an inland lake. It now had no water supply from below, it lay under a burning sun, and day by day evaporation carried it away.

The delta dam.

No one knows how many days, how many years, elapsed before the decrease of the water became noticeable. Doubtless the lake shrunk away slowly from the white face of the sand-dunes and the red walls of the mountains. The river-mouths that opened into the lake narrowed themselves to small stream - beds. The shelving beaches where the waves had fallen lazily year after year, pushing themselves over the sand in beautiful water-mirrors, shone bare and dry in the sunlight. The ragged reefs, over which the chop sea had tumbled and tossed so long, lifted their black hulks out

The inland lake.

of the water and with their hosts of barnacles and sea-life became a part of the land.

The first fall.

The waters of the great inland lake fell perhaps a hundred feet and then they made a pause. The exposed shores dried out. They baked hard in the sun, and were slowly ground down to sand and powdered silt by the action of the winds. The waters made a long pause. They were receiving reinforcements from some source. Possibly there was more rainfall in those days than now, and the streams entering the lake from the mountains were much larger. Again there may have been underground springs. There are flowing wells to-day in this old sea-bed—wells that cast up water salter than the sea itself. No one knows their fountain-head. Perhaps by underground channels the water creeps through from the Gulf, or comes from mountain reservoirs and turns saline by passing through beds of salt. These are the might-bes ; but it is far more probable that the Colorado River at high water had made a breach of some kind in the dam of its own construction and had poured overflow water into the lake by way of a dry channel called the New River. The bed of this river runs northward from below the boundary-line of Lower California ; and in 1893, during

Springs and wells in the sea-bed.

The New River.

a rise in the Colorado, the waters rushed in and flooded the whole of what is called the Salton Basin. When the Colorado receded, the basin soon dried out again.

It was undoubtedly some accident of this kind that called the halt in the original recession. During the interim the lake had time to form new shores where the waves pounded and washed on the gravel as before until miles upon miles of new beach—pebbled, shelled, and sloping downward with great uniformity—came into existence. This secondary beach is intact to-day and looks precisely like the primary except that it is not quite so large. Across the basin, along the southern mountains, the second water-tracery is almost as apparent as the first. The rocks are eaten in long lines by wave-action, and are honeycombed by the ceaseless energies of the zoöphite. *New beaches.*

Nor was the change in beach and rock alone. New bays and harbors were cut out from where the sea had been, new river-channels were opened down to the shrunken lake, new lagoons were spread over the flat places. Nature evidently made a great effort to repair the damage and adapt the lake to its new conditions. And the Indians, too, accepted the change. There *The second fall.*

are many indications in broken pottery, arrow-heads, and mortars that the aboriginal tribes moved down to the new beach and built wick-iups by the diminished waters. And the old fishing-foraging-fighting life was probably resumed.

Then once more the waters went down, down, down. Step by step they receded until the secondary beach was left a hundred feet above the water level. Again there was a pause. Again *The third beach.* new beaches were beaten into shape by the waves, new bays were opened, new arroyos cut through from above. The whole process of shore-making—the fitting of the land to the shrunken proportions of the lake — was gone through with for the third time ; while the water supply from the river or elsewhere was maintained in decreased volume but with some steadiness of flow. Possibly the third halt of the receding water was not for a great length of time. The tertiary beach is not so large as its predecessors. There never was any strong wave-*The failing water.* action upon it, its pebbles are few, its faults and breaks are many. The water supply was failing, and finally it ceased altogether.

What fate for a lake in the desert receiving no supplies from river or sea—what fate save annihilation ? The hot breath of the wind blew across the cramped water and whipped its surface into little waves ; and as each tiny point of spray rose on the crest and was lifted into the air the fiery sunbeam caught it, and in a twinkling had evaporated and carried it upward. Day by day this process went on over the whole surface until there was no more sea. The hollow reefs rose high and dark above the bed, the flat shoals of silt lifted out of the ooze, and down in the lowest pools there was the rush and plunge of monster tortuabas, sharks and porpoises, caught as it were in a net and vainly struggling to get out. How strange must have seemed that landscape when the low ridges were shining with the slime of the sea, when the beds were strewn with *algæ*, sponges, and coral, and the shores were whitening with salt ! How strange, indeed, must have been the first sight of the Bottom of the Bowl!

But the sun never relaxed its fierce heat nor the wind its hot breath. They scorched and burned the silt of the sea-bed until it baked and cracked into blocks. Then began the wear of the winds upon the broken edges until the blocks were reduced to dry fine powder. Finally the desert came in. Drifts upon drifts of

Evaporation.

Bottom of the Bowl.

Drying out of the sea-bed.

sand blown through the valleys settled in the
empty basin; gravel and bowlder-wash came
down from the mountains; the grease wood,
the salt-bush, and the so-called pepper-grass
sprang up in isolated spots. Slowly the desert
fastened itself upon the basin. Its heat became
Advance of desert. too intense to allow the falling rain to reach
the earth, its surface was too salt and alkaline
to allow of much vegetation, it could support
neither animal nor bird life; it became more
deserted than the desert itself.

And thus it remains to this day. When you
are in the bottom of it you are nearly three
Below sea-level. hundred feet below the level of the sea. Circling about you to the north, south, and west
are sierras, some of them over ten thousand feet
in height. These form the Rim of the Bowl.
And off to the southwest there is a side broken
out of the Bowl through which you can pass
to the river and the Gulf. The basin is perhaps
the hottest place to be found anywhere on the
Desolation of the basin. American deserts. And it is also the most forsaken. The bottom itself is, for the great part
of it, as flat as a table. It looks like a great
plain leading up and out to the horizon—a
plain that has been ploughed and rolled smooth.
The soil is drifted silt—the deposits made by

the washings from the mountains — and is almost as fine as flour.

The long line of dunes at the north are just as desolate, yet they are wonderfully beautiful. *Beauty of the sand-dunes.* The desert sand is finer than snow, and its curves and arches, as it builds its succession of drifts out and over an arroyo, are as graceful as the lines of running water. The dunes are always rhythmical and flowing in their forms; and for color the desert has nothing that surpasses them. In the early morning, before the sun is up, they are air-blue, reflecting the sky overhead; at noon they are pale lines of dazzling orange-colored light, waving and undulating in the heated air; at sunset they are often flooded with a rose or mauve color; under a blue moonlight they shine white as icebergs in the northern seas.

But neither the dunes nor the flats grow vegetation of consequence. About the high edges, up near the mountain slopes, you find growths of mesquite, palo verde, and cactus; *Cactus and salt-bush.* but down in the basin there are many miles where no weed or grass breaks the level uniformity. Not even the salt-bush will grow in some of the areas. And this is not due to poverty of soil but to absence of water and

intense heat. Plants cannot live by sunlight
alone.

Desert animals in the basin.

Nor will the desert animals inhabit an absolute waste. The coyote and the wildcat do not
relish life in this dip in the earth. They care
little for heat and drouth, but the question of
food appeals to them. There is nothing to eat.
Even the abstemious jack-rabbit finds living
here something of a difficulty. Many kinds of
tracks are found in the uncrusted silt—tracks
of coyotes, gray wolves, sometimes mountain
lions—but they all run in straight trails, showing the animals to be crossing the basin to the
mountains, not prowling or hunting. So, too,

Birds.

you will occasionally find birds—linnets, bobo-
links, mocking-birds, larks—but they are seen
one at a time, and they look weary-like land
birds far out at sea that seek a resting-place on
passing vessels. They do not belong to the
desert and are only stopping there temporarily

Lizards and snakes.

on some long flight. Snakes and lizards are not
particular about their abiding-place, and yet
they do not care to live in a land where there
is no bush or stone to creep under. You meet
with them very seldom. Practically there is no
life of any kind that is native to the place.

Is there any beauty, other than the dunes,

down in this hollow of the desert? Yes.
From a picturesque point of view it has the
most wonderful light, air, and color imaginable.
You will not think so until you see them
blended in that strange illusion known as
mirage. And here is the one place in all the *Mirage.*
world where the water-mirage appears to perfection. It does not show well over grassy or
bushy ground, but over the flat lake-beds of the
desert its appearance is astonishing. Down in
the basin it is accompanied by a second illusion *The water*
that makes the first more convincing. You *illusion.*
are below sea-level, but instead of the ground
about you sloping up and out, it apparently
slopes down and away on every side. You are
in the centre of a disk or high point of ground,
and around the circumference of the disk is
water—palpable, almost tangible, water. It
cannot be seen well from your horse, and fifty
feet up on a mountain side it would not be
visible at all. But dismount and you see it
better; kneel down and place your cheek to the
ground and now the water seems to creep up to
you. You could throw a stone into it. The
shore where the waves lap is just before you.
But where is the horizon-line? Odd enough,
this vast circling sea does not always know a

horizon; it sometimes reaches up and blends into the sky without any point of demarcation. Through the heated air you see faint outlines of mountains, dim glimpses of foot-hills, suggestions of distance; but no more. Across them is drawn the wavering veil of air, and the red earth at your feet, the blue sky overhead, are but bordering bands of flat color.

Decorative landscapes.

And there you have the most decorative landscape in the world, a landscape all color, a dream landscape. Painters for years have been trying to put it upon canvas—this landscape of color, light, and air, with form almost obliterated, merely suggested, given only as a hint of the mysterious. Men like Corot and Monet have told us, again and again, that in painting, clearly delineated forms of mountains, valleys, trees, and rivers, kill the fine color-sentiment of the picture. The great struggle of the modern landscapist is to get on with the least possible form and to suggest everything by tones of color, shades of light, drifts of air. Why? Because

Sensuous qualities in nature.

these are the most sensuous qualities in nature and in art. The landscape that is the simplest in form and the finest in color is by all odds the most beautiful. It is owing to just these features that this Bowl of the desert is a thing of

beauty instead of a dreary hollow in the hills.
Only one other scene is comparable to it, and
that the southern seas at sunset when the calm
ocean reflects and melts into the color-glory of
the sky. It is the same kind of beauty. Form
is almost blurred out in favor of color and air.

Yet here is more beauty destined to destruction. It might be thought that this forsaken
pot-hole in the ground would never come under
the dominion of man, that its very worthlessness *Changing*
would be its safeguard against civilization, that *the desert.*
none would want it, and everyone from necessity
would let it alone. But not even the spot deserted by reptiles shall escape the industry or the
avarice (as you please) of man. A great company
has been formed to turn the Colorado River
into the sands, to reclaim this desert basin, and
make it blossom as the rose. The water is to
be brought down to the basin by the old channel *Irrigation*
of the New River. Once in reservoirs it is to be *in the basin.*
distributed over the tract by irrigating ditches,
and it is said a million acres of desert will thus
be made arable, fitted for homesteads, ready for
the settler who never remains settled.

A most laudable enterprise, people will say.
Yes; commercially no one can find fault with
it. Money made from sand is likely to be clean

money, at any rate. And economically these acres will produce large supplies of food. That is commendable, too, even if those for whom it is produced waste a good half of what they already possess. And yet the food that is produced there may prove expensive to people other than the producers. This old sea-bed is, for its area, probably the greatest dry-heat generator in the world because of its depression and its barren, sandy surface. It is a furnace that whirls heat up and out of the Bowl, over the peaks of the Coast Range into Southern California, and eastward across the plains to Arizona and Sonora. In what measure it is responsible for the general climate of those States cannot be accurately summarized ; but it certainly has a great influence, especially in the

matter of producing dry air. To turn this desert into an agricultural tract would be to increase humidity, and that would be practically to nullify the finest air on the continent.

And why are not good air and climate as essential to human well-being as good beef and good bread ? Just now, when it is a world too late, our Government and the forestry societies of the country are awakening to the necessity of preserving the forests. National parks are being created wherever possible and the cutting of timber within them is prohibited. Why is this being done? Ostensibly to preserve the trees, but in reality to preserve the water supply, to keep the fountain-heads pure, to maintain a uniform stage of water in the rivers. Very proper and right. The only pity is that it was not undertaken forty years ago. But how is the water supply, from an economic and hygienic stand-point, any more important than the air supply?

Value of the air supply.

Grasses, trees, shrubs, growing grain, they, too, may need good air as well as human lungs. The deserts are not worthless wastes. You cannot crop all creation with wheat and alfalfa. Some sections must lie fallow that other sections may produce. Who shall say that the preternatural productiveness of California is not due to the warm air of its surrounding deserts? Does anyone doubt that the healthfulness of the countries lying west of the Mississippi may be traced directly to the dry air and heat of the deserts. They furnish health to the human; why not strength to the plant? The deserts should never be reclaimed. They are the breathing-spaces of the west and should be preserved forever.

Value of the deserts.

To speak about sparing anything because it is beautiful is to waste one's breath and incur ridicule in the bargain. The æsthetic sense—the power to enjoy through the eye, the ear, and the imagination—is just as important a factor in the scheme of human happiness as the corporeal sense of eating and drinking ; but there has never been a time when the world would admit it. The "practical men," who seem forever on the throne, know very well that beauty is only meant for lovers and young persons — stuff to suckle fools withal. The main affair of life is to get the dollar, and if there is any money in cutting the throat of Beauty, why, by all means, cut her throat. That is what the "practical men" have been doing ever since the world began. It is not necessary to dig up ancient history ; for have we not seen, here in California and Oregon, in our own time, the destruction of the fairest valleys the sun ever shone upon by placer and hydraulic mining ? Have we not seen in Minnesota and Wisconsin the mightiest forests that ever raised head to the sky slashed to pieces by the axe and turned into a waste of tree-stumps and fallen timber ? Have we not seen the Upper Mississippi, by the destruction of

Destruction of natural beauty.

Effects of mining, lumbering, agriculture.

the forests, changed from a broad, majestic river into a shallow, muddy stream; and the beautiful prairies of Dakota turned under by the plough and then allowed to run to weeds? Men must have coal though they ruin the valleys and blacken the streams of Pennsylvania, they must have oil though they disfigure half of Ohio and Indiana, they must have copper if they wreck all the mountains of Montana and Arizona, and they must have gold though they blow Alaska into the Behring Sea. It is more than possible that the "practical men" have gained much practice and many dollars by flaying the fair face of these United States. They have stripped the land of its robes of beauty, and what have they given in its place? Weeds, wire fences, oil-derricks, board shanties and board towns—things that not even a "practical man" can do less than curse at.

Ploughing the prairies.

"Practical men"

And at last they have turned to the desert! It remains to be seen what they will do with it. Reclaiming a waste may not be so easy as breaking a prairie or cutting down a forest. And Nature will not always be driven from her purpose. Wind, sand, and heat on Sahara have proven hard forces to fight against; they

Fighting wind, sand, and heat.

may prove no less potent on the Colorado. And sooner or later Nature will surely come to her own again. Nothing human is of long duration. Men and their deeds are obliterated, *Nature eternal.* the race itself fades ; but Nature goes calmly on with her projects. She works not for man's enjoyment, but for her own satisfaction and her own glory. She made the fat lands of the earth with all their fruits and flowers and foliage ; and with no less care she made the desert with its sands and cacti. She intended that each should remain as she made it. When the locust swarm has passed, the flowers and grasses will return to the valley ; when man is gone, the sand and the heat will come back *Return of desolation.* to the desert. The desolation of the kingdom will live again, and down in the Bottom of the Bowl the opalescent mirage will waver skyward on wings of light, serene in its solitude, though no human eye sees nor human tongue speaks its loveliness.

CHAPTER IV

THE SILENT RIVER

THE career of the Colorado, from its rise in the Wind River Mountains in Wyoming to its final disappearance in the Gulf of California, seems almost tragic in its swift transitions. It starts out so cheerily upon its course ; it is so clear and pure, so sparkling with sunshine and spirit. It dashes down mountain valleys, gurgles under bowlders, swirls over waterfalls, flashes through ravines and gorges. With its sweep and glide and its silvery laugh it seems to lead a merry life. But too soon it plunges into precipitous canyons and enters upon its fierce struggle with the encompassing rock. Now it boils and foams, leaps and strikes, thunders and shatters. For hundreds of miles it wears and worries and undermines the rock to its destruction. During the long centuries it has cut down into the crust of the earth five thousand feet. But ever the stout walls keep casting it back, keep churning it into bubbles, beating it

Rise of the Colorado.

In the canyon.

into froth. At last, its canyon course run, exhausted and helpless, it is pushed through the escarpments, thrust out upon the desert, to find its way to the sea as best it can. Its spirit is broken, its vivacity is extinguished, its color is deepened to a dark red—the trail of blood that leads up to the death. Wearily now it drifts across the desert without a ripple, without a moan. Like a wounded snake it drags its length far down the long wastes of sand to where the blue waves are flashing on the Californian Gulf. And there it meets—obliteration.

On the desert.

After the clash and roar of the conflict in the canyons how impressive seems the stillness of the desert, how appalling the unbroken silence of the lower river ! Day after day it moves seaward, but without a sound. You start at its banks to find no waves, no wash upon gravel beaches, no rush of water over shoals. Instead of the soothing murmur of breaking falls there is at times the boil of currents from below— waters flung up sullenly and soon flattened into drifting nothingness by their own weight.

The lower river.

And how heavily the stream moves ! Its load of silt is gradually settling to the bottom, yet still the water seems to drag upon the shores. Every reef of sand, every island of mud, every overhanging willow or cottonwood or handful of arrow-weed holds out a restraining hand. But slowly, patiently, winding about obstructions, cutting out new channels, creeping where it may not run, the bubbleless water works its way to the sea. The night-winds steal along its shores and pass in and out among its sedges, but there are no whispering voices; and the stars emerge and shine upon the flat floor of water, but there is no lustre. The drear desolation of it! The blare of morning sunlight does not lift the pall, nor the waving illusions of the mirage break the stillness. The Silent River moves on carrying desolation with it; and at every step the waters grow darker, darker with the stain of red—red the hue of decay.

Sluggish movement.

Stillness of river.

It was not through paucity of imagination that the old Spaniards gave the name—Colorado.* During the first fifty years after its discovery the river was christened many times, but the name that finally clung to it was the one that gave accurate and truthful description.

The river's name.

* Colorado is said to be the Spanish translation of the Piman name *buqui aquimuti*, according to the late Dr. Elliot Coues; but the Spanish word was so obviously used to denote the red color of the stream, that any translation from the Indian would seem superfluous.

You may see on the face of the globe numerous muddy Missouris, blue Rhones, and yellow
Tibers ; but there is only one red river and that
the Colorado. It is not exactly an earthy red,
not the color of shale and clay mixed ; but the
red of peroxide of iron and copper, the *sang-du-*
bœuf red of oriental ceramics, the deep insistent
red of things time-worn beyond memory. And

Its red
color.

there is more than a veneer about the color. It
has a depth that seems luminous and yet is sadly
deceptive. You do not see below the surface
no matter how long you gaze into it. As well
try to see through a stratum of porphyry as
through that water to the bottom of the river.

To call it a river of blood would be exaggeration, and yet the truth lies in the exaggeration.
As one walks along its crumbling banks there is
the thought of that other river that changed its
hue under the outstretched rod of the prophet.

Compared
with the
Nile.

How weird indeed must have been the ensan-
guined flow of the Nile, with its little waves
breaking in crests of pink foam ! How strange
the shores where the receding waters left upon
sand and rock a bordering line of scarlet froth !
But the Colorado is not quite like that—not
so ghastly, not so unearthly. It may suggest
at times the heavy welling flow of thickening

blood which the sands at every step are trying to drink up; but this is suggestion only, not realization. It seems to hint at blood, and under starlight to resemble it; but the resemblance is more apparent than real. The Colorado is a red river but not a scarlet one.

The blood hue.

It may be thought odd that the river should change so radically from the clear blue-green of its fountain-head to the opaque red of its desert stream, but rivers when they go wandering down to the sea usually leave their mountain purity behind them. The Colorado rushing through a thousand miles of canyons, cuts and carries seaward with it red sands of shale, granite, and porphyry, red rustings of iron, red grits of carnelian, agate and garnet. All the tributaries come bearing their tokens of red copper, and with the rains the whole red surface of the watershed apparently washes into the smaller creeks and thus into the valleys. When the river reaches the desert carrying its burden of silt, it no longer knows the bowlder-bed, the rocky shores, the breaking waterfalls that clarify a stream. And there are no large pools where the water can rest while the silt settles to the bottom. Besides, the desert itself at times pours into the river an even

River changes.

Red sands and silt.

deeper red than the canyons. And it does this not through arroyos alone, but also by a wide surface drainage.

Often the slope of the desert to the river is gradual for many miles—sometimes like the top of a huge table slightly tilted from the horizontal. When the edge of the table is reached the mesa begins to break into terraces (often cut through by small gullies), and the final descent is not unlike the steps of a Roman circus leading down into the arena. During cloud-bursts the waters pour down these steps with great fury and the river simply acts as a catch-basin for all the running color of the desert.

River-banks.

The " bottom " lands, forming the immediate banks of the river, are the silt deposits of former years. Often they are several miles in width and are usually covered with arrow-weed, willows, alders, and cottonwoods. The growth is dense if not tall and often forms an almost impenetrable jungle through which are scattered little openings where grass and flowers grow and Indians build reed wickiups and raise melons and corn in season. The desert terraces on either side (sometimes there is a row of sand-dunes) come down to meet these "bottom" lands,

" Bottom " lands.

and the line where the one leaves off and the other begins is drawn as with the sharp edge of a knife. Seen from the distant mountain tops the river moves between two long ribbons of green, and the borders are the gray and gold mesas of the desert.

The green bands.

Afloat and drifting down between these lines of green your attention is perhaps not at first attracted by the water. You are interested in the thickets of alders and the occasional bursts of white and yellow flowers from among the bushes. They are very commonplace bushes, very ordinary flowers ; but how lovely they look as they seem to drift by the boat ! How silent again are these clumps of alder and willow ! There may be linnets and sparrows among them but they do not make their presence obtrusive in song. A hawk wheels along over the arrow-weed looking for quail, but his wings cut the air without noise. How deathly still everything seems ! The water wears into the soft banks, the banks keep sloughing into the stream, but again you hear no splashing fall.

Bushes and flowers.

And the water itself is just as soundless. There is never a sunken rock to make a little gurgle, never a strip of gravel beach where a wave could charm you with its play. The beat

Soundless water.

of oars breaks the air with a jar, but breaks no bubbles on the water. You look long at the stream and fall to wondering if there can be any life in it. What besides a polywog or a bullhead could live there? Obviously, and in fact—nothing. Perhaps there are otter and beaver living along the pockets in the banks? Yes; there were otter and beaver here at one time, but they are very scarce to-day. But *Wild fowl.* there are wild fowl? Yes; in the spring and fall the geese and ducks follow the river in their flights, but they do not like the red water. What proof? Because they do not stop long in any one place. They swing into a bayou or slough late at night and go out at early dawn. They do not love the stream, but wild fowl on their migratory flights must have water, and this river is the only one between the Rockies and the Pacific that runs north and south.

Herons and bitterns. The blue herons and the bitterns do not mind the red mud or the red water, in fact they rather like it; but they were always solitary people of the sedge. They prowl about the marshes alone and the swish of oars drives them into the air with a guttural "Quowk." And there are snipe here, bands of them, flashing their wings in the sun as they wheel over the red waters or trip along the muddy banks singly or in pairs. They are quite at home on the bars and bayou flats, but it seems not a very happy home for them—that is judging by the absence of snipe talk. The little teeter flies ahead of you from point to point, but makes no twitter, the yellow-leg seldom sounds his mellow three-note call, and the kill-deer, even though you shoot at him, will not cry " Kill-deer ! " " Kill-deer ! "

Snipe.

It may be the season when birds are mute, or it may merely happen so for to-day, or it may be that the silence of the river and the desert is an oppressive influence ; but certainly you have never seen bird-life so hopelessly sad. Even the kingfisher, swinging down in a blue line from a dead limb and skimming the water, makes none of that rattling clatter that you knew so well when you were a child by a New England mill-stream. And what does a king-fisher on such a river as this ? If it were filled with fish he could not see them through that thick water.

Sad bird-life.

The voiceless river ! From the canyon to the sea it flows through deserts, and ever the seal of silence is upon it. Even the scant life of its borders is dumb—birds with no note, animals

with no cry, human beings with no voice. And
so forsaken ! The largest river west of the
mountains and yet the least known. There are
miles upon miles of mesas stretching upward
from the stream that no feet have ever trodden,
and that possess not a vestige of life of any
kind. And along its banks the same tale is
told. You float for days and meet with no
traces of humanity. When they do appear it is
but to emphasize the solitude. An Indian
wickiup on the bank, an Indian town ; yes, a
white man's town, what impression do they
make upon the desert and its river ? You drift
by Yuma and wonder what it is doing there.
Had it been built in the middle of the Pacific
on a barren rock it could not be more isolated,
more hopelessly " at sea."

After the river crosses the border-line of
Mexico it grows broader and flatter than ever.
And still the color seems to deepen. For all its
suggestion of blood it is not an unlovely color.
On the contrary, that deep red contrasted with
the green of the banks and the blue of the sky,
makes a very beautiful color harmony. They
are hues of depth and substance—hues that
comport excellently well with the character of
the river itself. And never a river had more

*The
forsaken.*

Solitude.

*Beauty of
the river.*

character than the Colorado. You may not
fancy the solitude of the stream nor its sugges-
tive coloring, but you cannot deny its majesty *Its majesty.*
and its nobility. It has not now the babble of
the brook nor the swift rush of the canyon
water ; rather the quiet dignity that is above
conflict, beyond gayety. It has grown old, it
is nearing its end ; but nothing could be calmer,
simpler, more sublime, than the drift of it down
into the delta basin.

The mountains are receding on every side,
the desert is flattening to meet the sea, and the
ocean tides are rising to meet the river. Half
human in its dissolution, the river begins to
break joint by joint. The change has been
gradually taking place for miles and now mani-
fests itself positively. The bottom lands widen,
many channels or side-sloughs open upon the
stream, and the water is distributed into the
mouths of the delta. There is a break in the *The delta.*
volume and mass—a disintegration of forces. *Disintegra-*
And by divers ways, devious and slow, the *tion.*
crippled streams well out to the Gulf and never
come together again.

It is not so when the river is at its height with
spring freshets. Then the stream is swollen
beyond its banks. All the bottom lands for

miles across, up to the very terraces of the mesas, are covered ; and the red flood moves like an ocean current, vast in width, ponderous in weight, irresistible in strength. All things that can be uprooted or wrenched away, move with it. Nothing can check or stop it now. It is the Grand Canyon river once more, free, mighty, dangerous even in its death-throes.

The river during floods.

And now at the full and the change of the moon, when the Gulf waters come in like a tidal wave, and the waters of the north meet the waters of the south, there is a mighty conflict of opposing forces. The famous "bore" of the river-mouth is the result. When the forces first meet there is a slow push-up of the water which rises in the shape of a ridge or wedge. The sea-water gradually proves itself the greater and the stronger body, and the ridge breaks into a crest and pitches forward with a roar. The undercut of the river sweeps away the footing of the tide, so to speak, and flings the top of the wave violently forward. The red river rushes under, the blue tide rushes over. There is the flash and dash of parti-colored foam on the crests, the flinging of jets of spray high in air, the long roll of waves breaking not upon a beach, but upon the back of the river,

The "bore."

Meeting of river and sea.

and the shaking of the ground as though an earthquake were passing. After it is all done with and gone, with no trace of wave or foam remaining, miles away down the Gulf the red river slowly rises in little streams through the blue to the surface. There it spreads fan-like over the top of the sea, and finally mingles with and is lost in the greater body.

The river is no more. It has gone down to its blue tomb in the Gulf—the fairest tomb that ever river knew. Something of serenity in the Gulf waters, something of the monumental in the bordering mountains, something of the unknown and the undiscovered over all, make it a fit resting-place for the majestic Colorado. The lonely stream that so shunned contact with man, that dug its bed thousands of feet in the depths of pathless canyons, and trailed its length across trackless deserts, sought out instinctively a point of disappearance far from the madding crowd. The blue waters of the Gulf, the beaches of shell, the red, red mountains standing with their feet in the sea, are still far removed from civilization's touch. There are no towns or roads or people by those shores, there are no ships upon those seas, there are no dust and smoke of factories in those skies. The Indians

The blue tomb.

Shores of the Gulf.

are there as undisturbed as in the days of
Coronado, and the white man is coming but
has not yet arrived. The sun still shines on
unknown bays and unexplored peaks. Therefore is there silence—something of the hush of
the deserts and the river that flows between.

CHAPTER V

LIGHT, AIR, AND COLOR

THESE deserts, cut through from north to south by a silent river and from east to west by two noisy railways, seem remarkable for only a few commonplace things, according to the consensus of public opinion. All that one hears or reads about them is that they are very hot, that the sunlight is very glaring, and that there is a sand-storm, a thirst, and death waiting for every traveller who ventures over the first divide.

Popular ideas of the desert.

There is truth enough, to be sure, in the heat and glare part of it, and an exceptional truth in the other part of it. It is intensely hot on the desert at times, but the sun is not responsible for it precisely in the manner alleged. The heat that one feels is not direct sunlight so much as radiation from the receptive sands; and the glare is due not to preternatural brightness in the sunbeam, but to there being no reliefs for the eye in shadows, in dark colors, in

Sunlight on desert.

heavy foliage. The vegetation of the desert is so slight that practically the whole surface of the sand acts as a reflector ; and it is this, rather than the sun's intensity, that causes the great body of light. The white roads in Southern France, for the surface they cover, are more glaring than any desert sands ; and the sunlight upon snow in Minnesota or New England is more dazzling. In certain spots where there

Glare and heat. are salt or soda beds the combination of heat and light is bewildering enough for anyone ; but such places are rare. White is something seldom seen on desert lands, and black is an unknown quantity in my observations. Even lava, which is popularly supposed to be as black as coal, has a reddish hue about it. Everything has some color—even the air. Indeed, we shall not comprehend the desert light without a momentary study of this desert air.

The circumambient medium which we call the atmosphere is to the earth only as so much ground-glass globe to a lamp—something that breaks, checks, and diffuses the light. We have

Pure sunlight. never known, never shall know, direct sunlight —that is, sunlight in its purity undisturbed by atmospheric conditions. It is a blue shaft falling perfectly straight, not a diffused white or yellow light ; and probably the life of the earth would not endure for an hour if submitted to its unchecked intensity. The white or yellow light, known to us as sunlight, is produced by the ground-glass globe of air, and it follows readily enough that its intensity is absolutely dependent upon the density of the atmosphere —the thickness of the globe. The cause for the thickening of the aërial envelope lies in the particles of dust, soot, smoke, salt, and vapor which are found floating in larger or smaller proportions in all atmospheres.

Atmospher-ic envelope.

In rainy countries like England and Holland the vapor particles alone are sufficiently numerous to cause at times great obscurity of light, as in the case of fog ; and the air is only comparatively clear even when the skies are all blue. The light is almost always whitish, and the horizons often milky white. The air is thick, for you cannot see a mountain fifteen miles away in any sharpness of detail. There is a mistiness about the rock masses and a vagueness about the outline. An opera-glass does not help your vision. The obscurity is not in the eyes but in the atmospheric veil through which you are striving to see. On the contrary, in the high plateau country of Wyoming, where

Vapor particles.

Clear air.

the quantities of dust and vapor in the air are comparatively small, the distances that one can see are enormous. A mountain seventy miles away often appears sharp-cut against the sky, and at sunset the lights and shadows upon its sides look only ten miles distant.

But desert air is not quite like the plateau air of Wyoming, though one can see through it for many leagues. It is not thickened by moisture particles, for its humidity is almost nothing ; but the dust particles, carried upward by radiation and the winds, answer a similar purpose. They parry the sunshaft, break and color the light, increase the density of the envelope. Dust is always present in the desert air in some degree, and when it is at its maximum with the heat and winds of July, we see the air as a blue, yellow, or pink haze. This haze is not seen so well at noonday as at evening when the sun's rays are streaming through canyons, or at dawn when it lies in the mountain shadows and reflects the blue sky. Nor does it muffle or obscure so much as the moisture-laden mists of Holland, but it thickens the air perceptibly and decreases in measure the intensity of the light.

Dust particles.

Hazes.

Yet despite the fact that desert air is dust-laden and must be thickened somewhat, there

is something almost inexplicable about it. It
seems so thin, so rarefied; and it is so scentless—I had almost said breathless—that it is
like no air at all. You breathe it without feel-
ing it, you look through it without being con- *Seeing the desert air.*
scious of its presence. Yet here comes in the
contradiction. Desert air is very easily recognized by the eyes alone. The traveller in California when he wakes in the morning and
glances out of the car-window at the air in the
mountain canyons, knows instantly on which
side of the Tehachepi Range the train is moving. He knows he is crossing the Mojave.
The lilac-blue veiling that hangs about those
mountains is as recognizable as the sea air of
the Massachusetts shore. And, strange enough,
the sea breezes that blow across the deserts all *Sea breezes on desert.*
down the Pacific coast have no appreciable ef-
fect upon this air. The peninsula of Lower
California is practically surrounded by water,
but through its entire length and down the
shores of Sonora to Mazatlan, there is nothing
but that clear, dry air.

I use the word "clear" because one can see
so far through this atmosphere, and yet it is
not clear or we should not see it so plainly.
There is the contradiction again. Is it perhaps

Colored air. the coloring of it that makes it so apparent ? Probably. Even the clearest atmosphere has some coloring about it. Usually it is an indefinable blue. Air-blue means the most delicate of all colors—something not of surface depth but of transparency, builded up by superimposed strata of air many miles perhaps in thickness. This air-blue is seen at its best in the gorges of the Alps, and in the mountain distances of Scotland ; but it is not so apparent on the desert. The coloring of the atmosphere

Different hues. on the Colorado and the Mojave is oftener pink, yellow, lilac, rose-color, sometimes fire-red. And to understand that we must take up the ground-glass globe again.

It has been said that our atmosphere breaks, checks, and diffuses the falling sunlight like the globe of a lamp. It does something more. It acts as a prism and breaks the beam of sun-

Producing color. light into the colors of the spectrum. Some of these colors it deals with more harshly than others because of their shortness and their weakness. The blue rays, for instance, are the greatest in number ; but they are the shortest in length, the weakest in travelling power of any of them. Because of their weakness, and because of their affinity (as regards size) with

the small dust particles of the higher air region, great quantities of these rays are caught,
refracted, and practically held in check in the
upper strata of the atmosphere. We see them
massed together overhead and call them the
"blue sky." After many millions of these
blue rays have been eliminated from the sunlight the remaining rays come down to earth
as a white or yellow or at times reddish light,
dependent upon the density of the lower atmosphere.

*Refracted
rays.*

Now it seems that an atmosphere laden with
moisture particles obstructs the passage earthward of the blue rays, less perhaps than an
atmosphere laden with dust. In consequence,
when they are thus allowed to come down into
the lower atmosphere in company with the
other rays, their vast number serves to dom-
inate the others, and to produce a cool tone of
color over all. So it is that in moist countries
like Scotland you will find the sky cold-blue
and the air tinged gray, pale-blue, or at twilight in the mountain valleys, a chilly purple.
A dust-laden atmosphere seems to act just the
reverse of this. It obstructs all the rays in
proportion to its density, but it stops the blue
rays first, holds them in the upper air, while

*Cold colors,
how
produced.*

Warm
colors.

the stronger rays of red and yellow are only
checked in the lower and thicker air-strata
near the earth. The result of this is to produce a warm tone of color over all. So it is
that in dry countries like Spain and Morocco
or on the deserts of Africa and America, you
will find the sky rose-hued or yellow, and the
air lilac, pink, red, or yellow.

I mean now that the air itself is colored. Of
course countless quantities of light-beams and
dispersed rays break through the aërial envelope
and reach the earth, else we should not see
color in the trees or grasses or flowers about
us; but I am not now speaking of the color of
objects on the earth, but of the color of the air.
A thing too intangible for color you think?

Sky colors.

But what of the sky overhead? It is only tinted atmosphere. And what of the bright-hued
horizon skies at sunrise and sunset, the rosy-
yellow skies of Indian summer! They are only
tinted atmospheres again. Banked up in great
masses, and seen at long distances, the air-color
becomes palpably apparent. Why then should
it not be present in shorter distances, in mountain canyons, across mesas and lomas, and over
the stretches of the desert plains?

The truth is all air is colored, and that of

the desert is deeper dyed and warmer hued than
any other for the reasons just given. It takes
on many tints at different times, dependent
upon the thickening of the envelope by heat *Color pro-*
and dust-diffusing winds. I do not know if it *duced by dust.*
is possible for fine dust to radiate with heat
alone ; but certain it is that, without the aid of
the wind, there is more dust in the air on hot
days than at any other time. When the ther-
mometer rises above 100° F., the atmosphere is
heavy with it, and the lower strata are dancing
and trembling with phantoms of the mirage at
every point of the compass. It would seem as
though the rising heat took up with it countless *Effect of*
small dust-particles and that these were respon- *heat.*
sible for the rosy or golden quality of the air-
coloring.

There is a more positive tinting of the air
produced sometimes by high winds. The lighter *Effect of*
particles of sand are always being drifted here *winds.*
and there through the aërial regions, and even
on still days the whirlwinds are eddying and
circling, lifting long columns of dust skyward
and then allowing the dust to settle back to
earth through the atmosphere. The stronger
the wind, and the more of dust and sand, the
brighter the coloring. The climax is reached

in the dramatic sand-storm—a veritable sand-fog which often turns half the heavens into a luminous red, and makes the sun look like a round ball of fire.

The dust-particle in itself is sufficient to account for the warmth of coloring in the desert air—sufficient in itself to produce the pink, yellow, and lilac hazes. And yet I am tempted to suggest some other causes. It is not easy to prove that a reflection may be thrown upward upon the air by the yellow face of the desert beneath it—a reflection similar to that produced by a fire upon a night sky—yet I believe there is something of the desert's air-coloring derived from that source. Nor is it easy to prove that a reflection is cast by blue, pink, and yellow skies, upon the lower air-strata, yet certain effects shown in the mirage (the water illusion, for instance, which seems only the reflection of the sky from heated air) seem to suggest it. And if we put together other casual observations they will make argument toward the same goal. For instance, the common blue haze that we may see any day in the mountains, is always deepest in the early morning when the blue sky over it is deepest. At noon when the sky turns gray-blue the haze turns gray-blue also. The yellow haze of the desert is seen at its best when there is a yellow sunset, and the pink haze when there is a red sunset, indicating that at least the sky has some part in coloring by reflection the lower layers of desert air.

Blue, yellow, and pink hazes.

Whatever the cause, there can be no doubt about the effect. The desert air is practically colored air. Several times from high mountains I have seen it lying below me like an enormous tinted cloud or veil. A similar veiling of pink, lilac, or pale yellow is to be seen in the gorges of the Grand Canyon; it stretches across the Providence Mountains at noonday and is to be seen about the peaks and packed in the valleys at sunset; it is dense down in the Coahuila Basin; it is denser from range to range across the hollow of Death Valley; and it tinges the whole face of the Painted Desert in Arizona. In its milder manifestations it is always present, and during the summer months its appearance is often startling. By that I do not mean that one looks through it as through a highly colored glass. The impression should not be gained that this air is so rose-colored or saffron-hued that one has to rub his eyes and wonder if he is awake. The average unobservant traveller looks

The dust-veil.

Summer coloring.

through it and thinks it not different from any other air. But it is different. In itself, and in its effect upon the landscape, it is perhaps responsible for the greater part of what everyone calls "the wonderful color" of the desert.

Local hues.

And this not to the obliteration of local hue in sands, rocks, and plants. Quite independent of atmospheres, the porphyry mountains are dull red, the grease wood is dull green, the vast stretches of sand are dull yellow. And these large bodies of local color have their influence in the total sum-up. Slight as is the vegetation upon the desert, it is surprising how it seems to bunch together and count as a color-mass. Almost all the growths are "evergreen." The shrubs and the trees shed their leaves, to be sure, but they do it so slowly that the new ones are on before the old ones are off. The general

Greens of desert plants.

appearance is always green, but not a bright hue, except after prolonged rains. Usually it is an olive, bordering upon yellow. One can hardly estimate what a relieving note this thin thatch of color is, or how monotonous the desert might be without it. It is welcome, for it belongs to the scene, and fits in the color-scheme of the landscape as perfectly as the dark-green pines in the mountain scenery of Norway.

The sands, again, form vast fields of local color, and, indeed, the beds of sand and gravel, the dunes, the ridges, and the mesas, make up the most widespread local hue on the desert. The sands are not "golden," except under peculiar circumstances, such as when they are whirled high in the air by the winds, and then struck broadside by the sunlight. Lying quietly upon the earth they are usually a dull yellow. In the morning light they are often gray, at noon frequently a bleached yellow, and at sunset occasionally pink or saffron-hued. Wavering heat and mirage give them temporary coloring at times that is beautifully unreal. They then appear to undulate slightly like the smooth surface of a summer sea at sunset; and the colors shift and travel with the undulations. The appearance is not common; perfect calm, a flat plain, and intense heat being apparently the conditions necessary to its existence.

Color of sands.

Sands in mirage.

The rocks of the upper peaks and those that make the upright walls of mountains, though small in body of color, are perhaps more varied in hue than either the sands or the vegetation, and that, too, without primary notes as in the

Color of
mountain
walls.

Grand Canyon of the Yellowstone. The reds are
always salmon-colored, terra-cotta, or Indian
red; the greens are olive-hued, plum-colored,
sage-green; the yellows are as pallid as the
leaves of yellow roses. Fresh breaks in the
wall of rock may show brighter colors that
have not yet been weather-worn, or they may
reveal the oxidation of various minerals. Often
long strata and beds, and even whole mountain
tops show blue and green with copper, or
orange with iron, or purple with slates, or white
with quartz. But the tones soon become subdued. A mountain wall may be dark red within, but it is weather-stained and lichen-covered
without; long-reaching shafts of granite that
loom upward from a peak may be yellow at
heart but they are silver-gray on the surface.
The colors have undergone years of " toning
down " until they blend and run together like
the faded tints of an Eastern rug.

Weather
staining.

But granted the quantity and the quality of
local colors in the desert, and the fact still remains that the air is the medium that influ-
ences if it does not radically change them all.
The local hue of a sierra may be gray, dark red,
iron-hued, or lead-colored ; but at a distance,
seen through dust-laden air, it may appear

Influence of
the air.

topaz-yellow, sapphire-blue, bright lilac, rose-red—yes, fire-red. During the heated months of summer such colors are not exceptional. They appear almost every evening. I have seen at sunset, looking north from Sonora some twenty miles, the whole tower-like shaft of Baboqui-vari change from blue to topaz and from topaz to glowing red in the course of half an hour. I do not mean edgings or rims or spots of these colors upon the peak, but the whole upper half of the mountain completely changed by them. The red color gave the peak the appearance of hot iron, and when it finally died out the dark dull hue that came after was like that of a clouded garnet.

Peak of Baboqui-vari.

The high ranges along the western side of Arizona, and the buttes and tall spires in the Upper Basin region, all show these warm fire-colors under heat and sunset light, and often in the full of noon. The colored air in conjunction with light is always responsible for the hues. Even when you are close up to the moun-tains you can see the effect of the air in small ways. There are edgings of bright color to the hill-ridges and the peaks ; and in the canyons, where perhaps a sunshaft streams across the shadow, you can see the gold or fire-color of the

Buttes and spires.

Sunshafts
through
canyons.

air most distinctly. Very beautiful are these golden sunshafts shot through the canyons. And the red shafts are often startling. It would seem as though the canyons were packed thick with yellow or red haze. And so in reality they are.

There is one marked departure from the uniform warm colors of the desert that should be mentioned just here. It is the clear blue seen in the shadows of western-lying mountains at sunset. This colored shadow shows only when there is a yellow or orange hued sunset, and it is produced by the yellow of the sky casting its

Comple-
mentary
hues in
shadow.

complementary hue (blue) in the shadow. At sea a ship crossing a yellow sunset will show a marvellous blue in her sails just as she crosses the line of the sun, and the desert mountains repeat the same complementary color with equal facility and greater variety. It is not of long duration. It changes as the sky changes, but maintains always the complementary hue.

The presence of the complementary color in the shadow is exceptional, however. The shadows cast by such objects as the sahuaro and the

Colored
shadows,

palo verde are apparently quite colorless; and so, too, are the shadows of passing clouds. The colored shadow is produced by reflection from the sky, mixed with something of local color in the background, and also complementary color. It is usually blue or lilac-blue, on snow for example, when there is a blue sky overhead ; and lilac when shown upon sand or a blue stone road. Perhaps it does not appear often on the Mojave-Colorado because the surfaces are too rough and broken with coarse gravel to make good reflectors of the sky. The fault is not in the light or in the sky, for upon the fine sands of the dunes, and upon beds of fine gypsum and salt, you can see your own shadow colored an absolute indigo ; and often upon bowlders of *Blue shad-* white quartz the shadows of cholla and grease *ows upon* *salt-beds.* wood are cast in almost cobalt hues.

All color—local, reflected, translucent, complementary—is, of course, made possible by light and has no existence apart from it. Through the long desert day the sunbeams are *How light* weaving skeins of color across the sands, along *makes color.* the sides of the canyons, and about the tops of the mountains. They stain the ledges of copper with turquoise, they burn the buttes to a terra-cotta red, they paint the sands with rose and violet, and they key the air to the hue of the opal. The reek of color that splashes the western sky at sunset is but the climax of the

*Desert
sunsets.*

sun's endeavor. If there are clouds stretched across the west the ending is usually one of exceptional brilliancy. The reds are all scarlet, the yellows are like burnished brass, the oranges like shining gold.

But the sky and clouds of the desert are of such unique splendor that they call for a chapter of their own.

CHAPTER VI

DESERT SKY AND CLOUDS

How silently, even swiftly, the days glide by
out in the desert, in the waste, in the wilderness! How "the morning and the evening
make up the day" and the purple shadow slips
in between with a midnight all stars! And
how day by day the interest grows in the long
overlooked commonplace things of nature! In
a few weeks we are studying bushes, bowlders,
stones, sand-drifts—things we never thought of
looking at in any other country. And after a
time we begin to make mental notes on the
changes of light, air, clouds, and blue sky. At
first we are perhaps bothered about the intensity of the sky, for we have always heard of the
"deep blue" that overhangs the desert; and
we expect to see it at any and all times. But
we discover that it shows itself in its greatest
depth only in the morning before sunrise. Then
it is a dark blue, bordering upon purple; and
for some time after the sun comes up it holds a

*Common-
place things
of nature.*

The blue sky. deep blue tinge. At noon it has passed through a whole gamut of tones and is pale blue, yellowish, lilac-toned, or rosy ; in the late afternoon it has changed again to pink or gold or orange ; and after twilight and under the moon, warm purples stretch across the whole reach of the firmament from horizon to horizon.

But the changes in the blue during the day have no constancy to a change. There is no fixed purpose about them. The caprices of light, heat, and dust control the appearances. *Changes in the blue.* Sometimes the sky at dawn is as pallid as a snowdrop with pearly grays just emerging from the blue ; and again it may be flushed with saffron, rose, and pink. When there are clouds and great heat the effect is often very brilliant. The colors are intense in chrome-yellows, golds, carmines, magentas, malachite-greens—a body of gorgeous hues upheld by enormous side wings of paler tints that encircle the horizon to the north and south, and send waves of color far up *Dawns on the desert.* the sky to the cool zenith. Such dawns are seldom seen in moist countries, nor are they usual on the desert, except during the hot summer months.

The prevailing note of the sky, the one oftenest seen, is, of course, blue—a color we may not perhaps linger over because it is so common. And yet how seldom it is appreciated! Our attention is called to it in art—in a hawthorn jar as large as a sugar-bowl, made in a certain period, in a certain Oriental school. The æsthetic world is perhaps set agog by this ceramic blue. But what are its depth and purity compared to the ethereal blue! Yet the color is beautiful in the jar and infinitely more beautiful in the sky—that is beautiful in itself and merely as color. It is not necessary that it should mean anything. Line and tint do not always require significance to be beautiful. There is no tale or text or testimony to be tortured out of the blue sky. It is a splendid body of color; no more.

Blue as a color.

You cannot always see the wonderful quality of this sky-blue from the desert valley, because it is disturbed by reflections, by sand-storms, by lower air strata. The report it makes of itself when you begin to gain altitude on a mountain's side is quite different. At four thousand feet the blue is certainly more positive, more intense, than at sea-level; at six thousand feet it begins to darken and deepen, and it seems to fit in the saddles and notches of the mountains like a block of lapis lazuli; at eight thousand feet it

Sky from mountain heights.

has darkened still more and has a violet hue about it. The night sky at this altitude is almost weird in its purples. A deep violet fits up close to the rim of the moon, and the orb itself looks like a silver wafer pasted upon the sky.

The night sky.

The darkening of the sky continues as the height increases. If one could rise to, say, fifty thousand feet, he would probably see the sun only as a shining point of light, and the firmament merely as a blue-black background. The diffusion of light must decrease with the growing thinness of the atmospheric envelope. At what point it would cease and the sky become perfectly black would be difficult to say, but certainly the limit would be reached when our atmosphere practically ceased to exist. Space from necessity must be black except where the straight beams of light stream from the sun and the stars.

Blackness of space.

The bright sky-colors, the spectacular effects, are not to be found high up in the blue of the dome. The air in the zenith is too thin, too free from dust, to take deep colorings of red and orange. Those colors belong near the earth, along the horizons where the aërial envelope is dense. The lower strata of atmosphere are in

Bright sky-colors.

fact responsible for the gorgeous sunsets, the tinted hazes, the Indian-summer skies, the hot September glows. These all appear in their splendor when the sun is near the horizon-line and its beams are falling through the many miles of hot, dust-laden air that lie along the surface of the earth. The air at sunset after a day of intense heat-radiation is usually so thick that only the long and strong waves of color can pass through it. The blues are almost lost, the neutral tints are missing, the greens are seen but faintly. The waves of red and yellow are the only ones that travel through the thick air with force. And these are the colors that tell us the story of the desert sunset. *Horizon skies.*

Ordinarily the sky at evening over the desert, when seen without clouds, shows the colors of the spectrum beginning with red at the bottom and running through the yellows, greens, and blues up to the purple of the zenith. In cool weather, however, this spectrum arrangement seems swept out of existence by a broad band of yellow-green that stretches half way around the circle. It is a pale yellow fading into a pale green, which in turn melts into a pale blue. In hot weather this pallor is changed to something much richer and deeper. A band *Spectrum colors.* *Bands of yellow.*

of orange takes its place. It is a flame-colored orange, and its hue is felt in reflection upon valley, plain, and mountain peak. This indeed is the orange light that converts the air in the mountain canyons into golden mist, and is measurably responsible for the yellow sunshafts that, streaming through the pinnacles of the western mountains, reach far across the upper sky in ever-widening bands. This great orange belt is lacking in that variety and vividness of coloring that comes with clouds, but it is not wanting in a splendor of its own. It is the broadest, the simplest, and in many respects the sublimest sunset imaginable—a golden dream with the sky enthroned in glory and the earth at its feet reflecting its lustre.

The orange sky.

But the more brilliant sunsets are only seen when there are broken translucent clouds in the west. There are cloudy days even on the desert. After many nights of heat, long skeins of white stratus will gather along the horizons, and out of them will slowly be woven forms of the cumulus and the nimbus. And it will rain in short squalls of great violence on the lomas, mesas, and bordering mountains. But usually the cloud that drenches a mountain top eight thousand feet up will pass over an

Desert clouds.

intervening valley, pouring down the same flood
of rain, and yet not a drop of it reaching the
ground. The air is always dry and the rain-
drop that has to fall through eight thousand   *Rainfall.*
feet of it before reaching the earth, never gets
there. It is evaporated and carried up to its
parent cloud again. During the so-called "rainy
season" you may frequently see clouds all about
the horizon and overhead that are "raining"
—letting down long tails and sheets of rain that
are plainly visible; but they never touch the
earth. The sheet lightens, breaks, and dissi-
pates two thousand feet up. It rains, true
enough, but there is no water, just as there are
desert rivers, but they have no visible stream.
That is the desert of it both above and below.

With the rain come trooping almost all the
cloud-forms known to the sky. And the thick
ones like the nimbus carry with them a chilling,   *Effect of the*
deadening effect. The rolls and sheets of rain-   *nimbus.*
clouds that cover the heavens at times rob the
desert of light, air, and color at one fell swoop.
Its beauty vanishes as by magic. Instead of
colored haze there is gray gloom settling along
the hills and about the mesas. The sands lose
their lustre and become dull and formless, the
vegetation darkens to a dead gray, and the

mountains turn slate-colored, mouldy, unwhole-
some looking. A mantle of drab envelops the
scene, and the glory of the desert has departed.

All the other cloud-forms, being more or less
transparent, seem to aid rather than to obscure
the splendor of the sky. The most common
Cumuli. clouds of all are the cumuli. In hot summer
afternoons they gather and heap up in huge
masses with turrets and domes of light that reach
at times forty thousand feet above the earth.
At sunset they begin to show color before any
of the other clouds. If seen against the sun
their edges at first gleam silver-white and then
change to gold ; if along the horizon to the
north or south, or lying back in the eastern sky,
they show dazzling white like a snowy Alp.
Heap clouds at sunset. As the sun disappears below the line they begin
to warm in color, turning yellow, pink, and rose.
Finally they darken into lilac and purple, then
sink and disappear entirely. The smaller forms
of cumulus that appear in the west at evening
are always splashes of sunset color, sometimes
being shot through with yellow or scarlet. They
ultimately appear floating against the night sky
as spots of purple and gray.

Above the cumuli and often flung across them
Strati. like bands of gauze, are the strati—clouds of

the middle air region. This veil or sheet-cloud
might be called a twilight cloud, giving out as
it does its greatest splendor after the sun has
disappeared below the verge. It then takes all
colors and with singular vividness. At times it
will overspread the whole west as a sheet of
brilliant magenta, but more frequently it blares
with scarlet, carmine, crimson, flushing up and
then fading out, shifting from one color to
another ; and finally dying out in a beautiful
ashes of roses. When these clouds and all their
variations have faded into lilac and deep purples, there are still bright spots of color in the
upper sky where the cirri are receiving the last
rays of the sun.

The cirrus with its many feathery and fleecy *Cirri.*
forms is the thinnest, the highest, and the most
brilliant in light of all the clouds. Perhaps its
brilliancy is due to its being an ice-cloud. It
seems odd that here in the desert with so much
heat rising and tempering the upper air there
should be clouds of ice but a few miles above it. *Ice-clouds.*
The cirrus and also the higher forms of the
cumulo-stratus are masses of hoar-frost, spicules
of ice floating in the air, instead of tiny glob-
ules of vapor.

There is nothing remarkable about the desert

clouds—that is nothing very different from the clouds of other countries—except in light, color, and background. They appear incomparably more brilliant and fiery here than elsewhere on the globe. The colors, like everything else on the desert, are intense in their power, fierce in their glare. They vibrate, they scintillate, they penetrate and tinge everything with their hue. And then, as though heaping splendor upon splendor, what a wonderful background they are woven upon ! Great bands of orange, green, and blue that all the melted and fused gems in the world could not match for translucent beauty. Taken as a whole, as a celestial tapestry, as a curtain of flame drawn between night and day, and what land or sky can rival it !

After the clouds have all shifted into purples and the western sky has sunk into night, then up from the east the moon — the misshapen orange-hued desert moon. How large it looks ! And how it warms the sky, and silvers the edges of the mountain peaks, and spreads its wide light across the sands ! Up, up it rises, losing something of its orange and gaining something in symmetry. In a few hours it is high in the heavens and has a great aureole of color about it. Look at the ring for a moment and you will

Clouds of fire.

The celestial tapestry.

The desert moon.

see all the spectrum colors arranged in order. Pale hues they are but they are all there. Rainbows by day and rainbows by night ! Radiant circles of colored light—not one but many. Arches above arches—not two or three but five solar bows in the sky at one time ! What strange tales come out of the wilderness ! But how much stranger, how much more weird and extraordinary the things that actually happen in this desert land.

Rings and rainbows.

High in the zenith rides the desert moon. What a flood of light comes from it ! What pale, phosphorescent light ! Under it miles and miles of cactus and grease wood are half revealed, half hidden ; and far away against the dark mountains the dunes of the desert shine white as snow-clad hills in December. The stars are forth, the constellations in their places, the planets large and luminous, yet none of them has much color or sparkle. The moon dims them somewhat, but even without the moon they have not the twinkle of the stars in higher, colder latitudes. The desert air seems to veil their lustre somewhat, and yet as points of light set in that purple dome of sky how beautiful they are !

Moonlight.

Stars.

Lying down there in the sands of the desert,

alone and at night, with a saddle for your pillow, and your eyes staring upward at the stars, how incomprehensible it all seems! The immensity and the mystery are appalling; and yet how these very features attract the thought and draw the curiosity of man. In the presence of the unattainable and the insurmountable we keep sending a hope, a doubt, a query, up through the realms of air to Saturn's throne. What key have we wherewith to unlock that door? We cannot comprehend a tiny flame of our own invention called electricity, yet we grope at the meaning of the blazing splendor of Arcturus. Around us stretches the great sand-wrapped desert whose mystery no man knows, and not even the Sphinx could reveal; yet beyond it, above it, upward still upward, we seek the mysteries of Orion and the Pleiades.

What is it that draws us to the boundless and the fathomless? Why should the lovely things of earth—the grasses, the trees, the lakes, the little hills — appear trivial and insignificant when we come face to face with the sea or the desert or the vastness of the midnight sky? Is it that the one is the tale of things known and the other merely a hint, a suggestion of the un-

The midnight sky.

Alone in the desert.

The mysteries.

known? Or have immensity, space, magnitude
a peculiar beauty of their own? Is it not true
that bulk and breadth are primary and essential qualities of the sublime in landscape? And
is it not the sublime that we feel in immensity
and mystery? If so, perhaps we have a partial
explanation of our love for sky and sea and
desert waste. They are the great elements.
We do not see, we hardly know if their boundaries are limited; we only feel their immensity, their mystery, and their beauty.

Space and immensity.

And quite as impressive as the mysteries are
the silences. Was there ever such a stillness as
that which rests upon the desert at night! Was
there ever such a hush as that which steals
from star to star across the firmament! You
perhaps think to break the spell by raising your
voice in a cry; but you will not do so again.
The sound goes but a little way and then seems
to come back to your ear with a suggestion of
insanity about it.

The silences.

A cry in the night! Overhead the planets
in their courses make no sound, the earth is
still, the very animals are mute. Why then the
cry of the human? How it jars the harmo-
nies! How it breaks in discord upon the uni-
ties of earth and air and sky! Century after

The cry of the human.

century that cry has gone up, mobbing high heaven ; and always insanity in the cry, insanity in the crier. What folly to protest where none shall hear ! There is no appeal from the law of nature. It was made for beast and bird and creeping thing. Will the human never learn that in the eye of the law he is not different from the things that creep ?

CHAPTER VII

ILLUSIONS

IN our studies of landscape we are very frequently made the victims of either illusion or delusion. The eye or the mind deceives us, and sometimes the two may join forces to our complete confusion. We are not willing to admit different reports of an appearance. The Anglo - Saxon in us insists that there can be only one truth, and everything else must be error. It is known, for instance, that Castle Dome, which looks down on the Colorado River from Western Arizona, is a turret of granite— gray, red, brown, rock-colored, whatever color you please. With that antecedent knowledge in mind how difficult it is for us to believe the report of our eyes which says that at sunset the dome is amethystine, golden, crimson, or perhaps lively purple. The reality is one thing, the appearance quite another thing ; but why are not both of them truthful ?

Reality and appearance.

And how very shy people are about accepting

109

a pink air, a blue shadow, or a field of yellow grass—sunlit lemon-yellow grass ! They have been brought up from youth to believe that air is colorless, that shadows are brown or gray or sooty black, and that grass is green—bottle-green. The preconceived impression of the mind refuses to make room for the actual impression of the eyes, and in consequence we are misled and deluded.

But do the eyes themselves always report the truth ? Yes ; the truth of appearances, but as regards the reality they may deceive you quite as completely as the mind deceives you about the apparent. And for the deception of the eyes there is no wizard's cell or magician's cabinet so admirably fitted for jugglery as this bare desert under sunlight. Its combination of light and air seem like reflecting mirrors that forever throw the misshapen image in unexpected places, in unexpected lights and colors.

What, for instance, could be more perplexing than the odd distortions in the forms and colors of the desert mountains ! A range of these mountains may often look abnormally grand, even majestic in the early morning as they stand against the eastern sky. The outlines of the ridges and peaks may be clear cut, the light

Pre-conceived impressions.

Deception by sunlight.

Distorted forms and colors.

and shade of the canyons and barrancas well marked, the cool morning colors of the face-walls and foot-hills distinctly placed and holding their proper value in the scene. But by noon the whole range has apparently lost its lines and shrunken in size. Under the beating rays of the sun and surrounded by wavering heated atmosphere its shadow masses have been grayed down, neutralized, perhaps totally obliterated ; and the long mountain surface appears as flat as a garden wall, as smooth as a row of sand-dunes. There is no indication of barranca or canyon. The air has a blue-steel glow that muffles light and completely wrecks color. Seen through it the escarpments show only dull blue and gray. All the reds, yellows, and pinks of the rocks are gone ; the surfaces wear a burnt-out aspect as though fire had eaten into them and left behind only a comb of volcanic ash.

Changed appearance of mountains.

At evening, however, the range seems to return to its majesty and magnitude. The peaks reach up, the bases broaden, the walls break into gashes, the ridges harden into profiles. The sun is westering, and the light falling more obliquely seems to bring out the shadows in the canyons and barrancas. Last of all the

Changes in line, light, and color.

colors come slowly back to their normal condition, as the flush of life to one recovering
from a trance. One by one they begin to glow
on chasm, wall, and needled summit. The air,
too, changes from steel-blue to yellow, from yellow to pink, from pink to lilac, until at last
with the sun on the rim of the earth, the mountains, the air, the clouds, and the sky are all
glowing with the tints of ruby, topaz, rose-dia-
mond—hues of splendor, of grandeur, of glory.

Suppose, if you please, a similar range of
mountains thirty miles away on the desert.
Even at long distance it shows an imposing
bulk against the sky, and you think if you were
close to it, wall and peak would loom colossal.
How surprised you are then as you ride toward
it, hour after hour, to find that it does not seem
to grow in size. When you reach the foot-hills
the high mountains seem little larger than when
seen at a distance. You are further surprised
that what appeared like a flat-faced range with
its bases touching an imaginary curb-stone for
miles, is in reality a group-range with retiring
mountains on either side that lead off on acute
angles. The group is round, and has as much
breadth as length. And still greater is your
surprise when you discover that the green top

of the gray-based mountain, which has been puzzling you for so many hours, does not belong to the gray base at all. It is a pine-clad top resting upon another and more massive base far back in the group. It is the highest and most central peak of the range.

Such illusions are common, easily explained ; and yet, after all, not so easily understood. They are caused by false perspective, which in turn is caused by light and air. On the desert, perspective is always erratic. Bodies fail to detach themselves one from another, foreshortening is abnormal, the planes of landscape are flattened out of shape or telescoped, objects are huddled together or superimposed one upon another. The disturbance in aërial perspective is just as bad. Colors, lights, and shadows fall into contradictions and denials, they shirk and bear false witness, and confuse the judgment of the most experienced.

False perspective.

Abnormal foreshortening.

Contradictions and denials.

No wonder amid this distortion of the natural, this wreck of perspective, that distance is such a proverbially unknown quantity. It is the one thing the desert dweller speaks about with caution. It may be thirty or fifty miles to that picacho—he is afraid to hazard a guess. If you should go up to the top of your mountain range

Deceptive distances.

and look at the valley beyond it, the distance
across might seem very slight. You can easily
see to where another mountain range begins
and trails away into the distance. Perhaps you
fancy a few hours' ride will take you over that
valley-plain to where the distant foot-hills are
lying soft and warm at the bases of the mountains. You may be right and then again you
may be wrong. You may spend two days getting to those foot-hills.

This deception of distance is not infrequently
accompanied by fatal consequences. The inex-
*Dangers of
the desert.* perienced traveller thinks the distance short, he
can easily get over the ground in a few hours.
But how the long leagues drag out, spin out,
reach out ! The day is gone and he is not
there, the slight supply of water is gone and
he is not there, his horse is gone and he himself
is going, but he is not there. The story and its
ending are familiar to those who live near the
desert, for every year some mining or exploring party is lost. If there are any survivors
they usually make the one report : "The distance seemed so short." But there are no short
*Immensity
of valley-
plains.* distances on the desert. Every valley-plain is
an immense wilderness of space.

There is another illusion—a harmless one—

that has not to do with perspective but with shadow and local color. The appearance is that of shadows cast down along the mountain's side by the ridges or hogbacks. Any little patch of shadow is welcome on the desert, particularly upon the mountains which are always so strongly flooded with light. But this is only a counterfeit presentment. The ridges have no vegetation upon them to hold in place the soil and rocks and these are continually breaking away into land-slips. The slips or slides expose to view streaks of local color such as may be seen in veins of iron and copper, in beds of lignite or layers of slate. It is these streaks and patches of dark color that have broken away and slipped down the mountain side under the ridges that give the appearance of shadows. They have the true value in light, and are fair to look upon even though they are deception. The weather-beaten rocks of a talus under a peak may create a similar illusion, but the shadow effect loses a velvety quality which it has when seen under the ridges.

The illusion of a cloud-shadow resting upon the foot-hills or in the valley, is frequently produced by the local color of lava-beds. Lava may be of almost any color, but when seen close

Shadow illusions.

Color-patches on mountains.

to view it is usually a reddish-black. At a distance, however, and as a mass, its beds have the exact value of a cloud-shadow. Any eye would be deceived by it. The great inundations of lava that have overrun the plains and oozed down the foot-hills and around the lomas (particularly on the Mojave) look the shadow to the very life. The beds are usually hedged about on all sides by banks of fine sand that seem to stand for sunlight surrounding the shadow, and thus the deception is materially augmented. Many times I have looked up at the sky to be sure there was no cloud there, so palpable is this lava shadow-illusion.

But perhaps the most beautiful deception known to the desert is the one oftenest seen —mirage. Everyone is more or less familiar with it, for it appears in some form wherever the air is heated, thickened, or has strata of different densities. It shows on the water, on the grass plains, over ploughed fields or gravel roads, on roadbeds of railways ; but the bare desert with its strong heat-radiation is primarily its home. The cause of its appearance —or at least one of its appearances—is familiar knowledge, but it may be well to state it in dictionary terms : " An optical illusion due to

Illusion of lava-beds.

Appearance of cloud-shadows.

Mirage.

Definition.

excessive bending of light-rays in traversing
adjacent layers of air of widely different densities, whereby distorted, displaced, or inverted
images are produced." *

This is no doubt the true explanation of that
form of mirage in which people on Sahara see
caravans in the sky trailing along, upside down,
like flies upon the ceiling ; or on the ocean see
ships hanging in the air, masts and sails downward. But the explanation is very general and
is itself in some need of explanation. Perhaps
then I may be pardoned for trying to illustrate
the theory of mirage in my own way.

*Need of ex-
planation.*

The rays of light that come from the sun to
the earth appear to travel in a straight line,
but they never do. As soon as they meet with
and pass into the atmospheric envelope they are
bent or deflected from their original direction
and reach the earth by obtuse angles or in long
descending curves like a spent rifle ball. This
bending of the rays is called refraction, which
must not be confounded with reflection—a something quite different. Now refraction is, of
course, the greatest where the atmosphere is the
densest. The thicker the air the more acute the
bending of the light-ray. Hence the thick lay-

*Refraction
of light-
rays.*

* Century Dictionary.

ers of air lying along or a few feet above the surface of the earth on a hot day are peculiarly well-fitted to distort the light-ray, and consequently well-fitted to produce the effect of mirage. These layers of air are of varying densities. Some are thicker than others; and in this respect the atmosphere bears a resemblance to an ordinary photographic or telescopic lens. Let us use the lens illustration for a moment and perhaps it will aid comprehension of the subject.

Dense air-strata.

You know that the lens, like the air, is of varying thicknesses or densities, and you know that in the ordinary camera the rays of light, passing through the upper part of the lens, are refracted or bent toward the perpendicular so that they reach the ground-glass "finder" at the bottom; and that the rays passing through the lower part of the lens go to the top of the "finder." The result is that you have on the "finder" or the negative something reversed—things upside down. That, so far as the reversed image goes, is precisely the case in mirage. The air-layers act as a lens and bend the light-rays so that when seen in our "finder" —the eye—the bottom of a tree, for example, goes to the top and the top goes to the bottom.

Illustration of camera lens.

But there is something more to mirage than this reversed image. The eyes do not see things "in their place," but see them hanging in the air as in the case of ships and caravans. To explain this, in the absence of a diagram, we shall have to take up another illustration. Suppose a light-ray so violently bent by the heat lying above a sidewalk that it should come to us around a street corner, and thereby we should see a man coming up a side street that lies at right angles to us. He would appear to our eyes to be coming up, not the side street, but the street we are standing in. The man, to all appearances, would not be " in his place." We should see him where he is not. *The bent light-ray.*

Now suppose again instead of the light-rays bending to right or left (as in the street-corner illustration), we consider them as bending skyward or earthward. Suppose yourself at sea and that you are looking up into the sky above the horizon. You see there a ship "out of its place," hanging in the air in an impossible manner—something which is equivalent, or at least analogous, to looking down the street and seeing the image of the man around the corner. You are looking straight into the sky, yet seeing a ship below the verge. The light-rays *Ships at sea.*

coming from the ship on the water describe an
obtuse angle or curve in reaching the eye. The
rays from the bottom of the ship, lying in a
dense part of the air-lens, are more acutely
bent than those from the masts, and hence they
go to the top of the photographic plate or your
field of vision, whereas the rays from the ship's
masts, being in a thinner atmosphere, are less
violently bent, and thus go to the bottom of your
field of vision. The result is the ship high in
Ships up-
side down. air above the horizon-line and upside down.

The illusion or deception consists in this :
We usually see things in flat trajectory, so to
speak. Light comes to us in comparatively
straight rays. The mind, therefore, has formu-
lated a law that we see only by straight rays.
Wherein the
illusion. In the case of mirage the light comes to us on
curved, bent, or angular rays. The eyes recog-
nize this, but the mind refuses to believe it and
hence is deceived. We think we see the ship
in the air by the straight ray, but in reality we
see the ship *on the water* by the bent ray. It
is thus that ships are often seen when far below
the horizon-line, and that islands in the sea below the ocean's rim, and so far away as a hundred miles, are seen looming in the air. " Looming " is the word that describes the excessive

apparent elevation of the object in the sky and
is more striking on sea than land. Captains of
vessels often tell strange tales of how high in
the air, ships and towns and coasts are seen.
The report has even come back from Alaska of
a city seen in the sky that is supposed to be the
city of Bristol. In tropical countries and over
warm ocean-currents there are often very acute
bendings of the light-rays. Why may it not be
so in colder lands with colder currents ?

"Looming" of vessels, islands, and cities.

The form of mirage that gives us the reversed
image is seen on the desert as well as on the
sea; but not frequently—at least not in my experience. There is an illusion of mountains
hanging peak downward from the sky, but one
may wander on the deserts for months and
never see it. The reality and the phantom
both appear in the view—the phantom seeming
to draw up and out of the original in a distorted, cloud-like shape. It is almost always
misshapen, and as it rises high in air it seems
to be detached from the original by currents of
air drifted in between. More familiar sights
are the appearances of trees, animals, houses,
wagons, all hanging in the air in enlarged and
elongated shapes and, of course, reversed. I
have seen horses hitched to a wagon hanging

Reversed image of mountains.

Horses and cattle in mirage.

high up in the air with the legs of the horses twenty feet long and the wagon as large as a cabin. The stilted antelope "forty feet high and upside down" is as seldom seen in the sky as upon the earth; but desert cattle in bunches of half a dozen will sometimes walk about on the aërial ceiling in a very astonishing way.

Yet these, too, are infrequent appearances.

Illusion of rising buttes.

Nor is the illusion of buttes rising from the plain in front of you often seen. It happens only when there are buttes at one side or the other, and, I presume, this mirage is caused by the bending of the light-rays to the right or left. It presents certainly a very beautiful effect. The buttes rise up from the ground, first one and then another, until there is a range of them that holds the appearance of reality perhaps for hours, and then gradually fades out like a stereopticon picture—the bases going first and the tops gradually melting into the sky. When seen at sunset against a yellow sky the effect is magnificent. The buttes, even in illusion, take on a wonderful blue hue (the complementary color of yellow), and they seem to drift upon the sky as upon an open sea.

The bending of the light-rays to either side

instead of up or down, as following the perpendicular, may or may not be of frequent occurrence. I do not even know if the butte appearance is to be attributed to that. The opportunity to see it came to me but once, and I had not then the time to observe whether the buttes in the mirage had sides the reverse of the originals. Besides, it is certain that mirage is caused in other ways than by the bending of light-rays. The most common illusion of the desert is the water-mirage and that is caused by reflection, not refraction. Its usual appearance is that of a lake or sea of water with what looks at a distance to be small islands in it. There are those with somewhat more lively imagination than their fellows who can see cows drinking in the water, trees along the margin of the shore (palms usually), and occasionally a farm-house, a ship, or a whale. I have never seen any of these wonderful things, but the water and island part of the illusion is to be seen almost anywhere in the desert basins during hot weather. In the lower portions of the Colorado it sometimes spreads over thousands of acres, and appears not to move for hours at a stretch. At other times the wavering of the heat or the swaying of the air strata, or a change in the

Other causes for mirage.

Water-mirage.

The lake appearance.

density of the air will give the appearance of waves or slight undulations on the water. In either case the illusion is quite perfect. Water lying in such a bed would reflect the exact color of the sky over it ; and what the eyes really see in this desert picture is the reflection of the sky not from water but from strata of thick air.

How produced.

This illusion of water is probably seen more perfectly in the great dry lake-beds of the desert where the ground is very flat and there is no vegetation, than elsewhere. In the old Coahuila Valley region of the Colorado the water comes up very close to you and the more you flatten the angle of reflection by flattening yourself upon the ground, the closer the water approaches. The objects in it which people imagine look like familiar things are certainly very near. And these objects—wild-fowl, bushes, tufts of swamp grass, islands, buttes—are frequently bewildering because some of them are right side up and some of them are not. Some are reversed in the air and some are quietly resting upon the ground.

Objects in the water.

It happens at times that the whole picture is confused by the light-rays being both reflected and refracted, and in addition that the rays from certain objects come to us in a direct line.

Confused mirage.

The ducks, reeds, and tufts of grass, for instance, are only clods of dirt or sand-banked bushes which are detached at the bottom by heavy drifts of air. We see their tops right side up by look-ing through the air-layer or some broken por-tion of it. But in the same scene there may be trees upside down, and mountains seen in re-flection, drawn out to stupendous proportions. In the Salton Basin one hot day in September a startled coyote very obligingly ran through a most brilliant water-mirage lying directly be-fore me. I could only see his head and part of his shoulders, for the rest of him was cut off by the air-layer ; but the appearance was that of a wolf swimming rapidly across a lake of water. *The swim-ming wolf.* The illusion of the water was exact enough be-cause it was produced by reflection, but there was no illusion about the upper part of the coyote. The rays of light from his head and shoulders came to me unrefracted and unre-flected—came as light usually travels from ob-ject to eye.

But refracted or reflected, every feature of the water-mirage is attractive. And sometimes its kaleidoscopic changes keep the fancy moving at a pretty pace. The appearance and disappear-ance of the objects and colors in the mirage

Colors and shadows in mirage.

are often quite wonderful.   The reversed mountain peaks, with light and shade and color upon them, wave in and out of the imaginary lake, and are perhaps succeeded by undulations of horizon colors in grays and pinks, by sunset skies and scarlet clouds, or possibly by the white cap of a distant sierra that has been caught in the angle of reflection.

But with all its natural look one is at loss to understand how it could ever be seriously accepted as a fact, save at the first blush.   People dying for water and in delirium run toward it —at least the more than twice-told tales of travellers so report—but I never knew any healthy eye that did not grow suspicious of it after the first glance.   It trembles and glows too much and soon reveals itself as something intangible, hardly of earth, little more than a shifting fantasy.   You cannot see it clear-cut and well-defined, and the snap-shot of your camera does not catch it at all.

Trembling air.

Yet its illusiveness adds to, rather than detracts from, its beauty.   Rose-colored dreams are always delightful ; and the mirage is only a dream.   It has no more substantial fabric than the golden haze that lies in the canyons at sunset.   It is only one of nature's veilings which she puts on or off capriciously. But again its *Beauty of mirage.* loveliness is not the less when its uncertain, fleeting character is revealed. It is one of the desert's most charming features because of its strange light and its softly glowing opaline color. And there we have come back again to that beauty in landscape which lies not in the lines of mountain valley and plain, but in the almost formless masses of color and light.

CHAPTER VIII

CACTUS AND GREASE WOOD

NATURE seems a benevolent or a malevolent goddess just as our own inadequate vision happens to see her. If we have eyes only for her creative beauties we think her all goodness; if we see only her power of destruction we incline to think she is all evil. With what infinite care and patience, worthy only of a good goddess, does she build up the child, the animal, the bird, the tree, the flower! How wonderfully she fits each for its purpose, rounding it with strength, energy, and grace; and beautifying it with a prodigality of colors. For twenty years she works night and day to bring the child to perfection, for twenty days she toils upon the burnished wings of some insect buzzing in the sunlight, for twenty hours she paints the gold upon the petals of the dandelion. And then what? What of the next twenty? Does she leave her handiwork to take care of itself until an unseen dragon called Decay comes

128

along to destroy it? Not at all. The good
goddess has a hand that builds up. Yes; and
she has another hand that takes down. The
marvellous skill of the one has its complement,
its counterpart, in the other. Block by block
she takes apart the mosaic with just as much
deftness as she put it together.

Growth and decay.

Those first twenty years of our life we were
allowed to sap blood and strength from our surroundings; the last twenty years of our life our
surroundings are allowed to sap blood and
strength from us. It is Nature's plan and it is
carried out without any feeling. With the same
indifferent spirit that she planted in us an eye
to see or an ear to hear, she afterward plants a
microbe to breed and a cancer to eat. She in
herself is both growth and decay. The virile
and healthy things of the earth are hers; and
so, too, are disease, dissolution, and death. The
flower and the grass spring up, they fade, they
wither; and Nature neither rejoices in the life
nor sorrows in the death. She is neither good
nor evil; she is only a great law of change that
passeth understanding. The gorgeous pagean-
try of the earth with all its beauty, the life
thereon with its hopes and fears and struggles,
and we a part of the universal whole, are brought

Nature's plan.

The law of change.

up from the dust to dance on the green in the sunlight for an hour; and then the procession that comes after us turns the sod and we creep back to Mother Earth. All, all to dust again; and no man to this day knoweth the why thereof.

One is continually assailed with queries of this sort whenever and wherever he begins to study Nature. He never ceases to wonder why *Nature foiling her own plans.* she should take such pains to foil her own plans and bring to naught her own creations. Why did she give the flying fish such a willowy tail and such long fins, why did she labor so industriously to give him power of flight, when at the same time she was giving another fish in the sea greater strength, and a bird in the air greater swiftness wherewith to destroy him? Why should she make the tarantula such a powerful engine of destruction when she was in the same hour making his destroyer, the tarantula-wasp? And always here in the desert the question comes up: Why should Nature give these shrubs and plants such powers of endurance and resistance, and then surround them by heat, *Attack and defence.* drouth, and the attacks of desert animals? It is existence for a day, but sooner or later the growth goes down and is beaten into dust.

The individual dies. Yes; but not the species.

Perhaps now we are coming closer to an understanding of Nature's method. It is the species that she designs to last, for a period at least; and the individual is of no great importance, merely a sustaining factor, one among millions requiring continual renewal. It is a small matter whether there are a thousand acres of grease wood more or less, but it is important that the family be not extinguished. It grows readily in the most barren spots, is very abundant and very hardy, and hence is protected only by an odor and a varnish. On the contrary take the bisnaga—a rather rare cactus. It has only a thin, short tap-root, therefore it has an enormous upper reservoir in which to store water, and a most formidable armor of fish-hook shaped spines that no beast or bird can penetrate. Remove the danger which threatens the extinction of the family and immediately Nature removes the defensive armor. On the desert, for instance, the yucca has a thorn like a point of steel. Follow it from the desert into the high tropical table-lands of Mexico where there is plenty of soil and moisture, plenty of chance for yuccas to thrive, and you will find it turned into a tree, and the thorn merely a dull blade-ending. Follow the sahuaro and the

Preservation of the species.

Means of preservation.

pitahaya into the tropics again, and with their
cousin, the organ cactus, you find them growing
a soft thorn that would hardly penetrate clothing. Abundance of soil and rain, abundance
of other vegetation for browsing animals, and
there is no longer need of protection. With
it the family would increase too rapidly.

So it seems that Nature desires neither increase nor decrease in the species. She wishes

*Maintain-
ing the
status quo.*
to maintain the *status quo*. And for the sake
of keeping up the general healthfulness and
virility of her species she requires that there
shall be change in the component parts. Each
must suffer not a "sea change," but a chemical
change ; and passing into liquids, gases, or dusts,
still from the grave help on the universal plan.
So it is that though Nature dips each one of her
desert growths into the Styx to make them in-
vulnerable, yet ever she holds them by the heel
and leaves one point open to the destroying
arrow.

*The plant-
struggle for
life.*
Yet it is remarkable how Nature designs and
prepares the contest — the struggle for life —
that is continually going on in her world. How
wonderfully she arms both offence and defence !
What grounds she chooses for the conflict !
What stern conditions she lays down ! Given a

waste of sand and rock, given a heat so intense
that under a summer sun the stones will blister
a bare foot like hot iron, given perhaps two or
three inches of rain in a twelvemonth ; and
what vegetation could one expect to find growing there ? Obviously, none at all. But
no ; Nature insists that something shall fight *Fighting heat and drouth.*
heat and drouth even here, and so she designs
strange growths that live a starved life, and
bring forth after their kind with much labor.
Hardiest of the hardy are these plants and just
as fierce in their way as the wild-cat. You cannot touch them for the claw. They have no
idea of dying without a struggle. You will
find every one of them admirably fitted to endure. They are marvellous engines of resistance.

The first thing that all these plants have to
fight against is heat, drouth, and the evaporation
of what little moisture they may have. And
here Nature has equipped them with ingenuity
and cunning. Not all are designed alike, to be
sure, but each after its kind is good. There
are the cacti, for example, that will grow where *Prevention of evapora-tion.*
everything else perishes. Why ? For one rea-
son because they have geometrical forms that
prevent loss from evaporation by contracting a

minimum surface for a given bulk of tissue.*
There is no waste, no unnecessary exposure of
surface.   Then there are some members of the
family like the "old man" cactus, that have
thick coatings of spines and long hairy growths
that prevent the evaporation of moisture by
keeping off the wind.   Then again the cacti
Absence of have no leaves to tempt the sun.   Many of the
large leaves. desert growths are so constructed.   Even such
a tree as the lluvia d'oro has needles rather than
leaves, though it does put forth a row of tiny
leaves near the end of the needle ; and when we
come to examine the ordinary trees such as the
mesquite, the depua, the palo breya, the palo
verde, and all the acacia family, we find they
have very narrow leaves that have a fashion of
hanging diagonally to the sun and thus avoiding the direct rays.   Nature is determined that
Exhaust of there shall be no unnecessary exhaust of moist-
moisture. ure through foliage.   The large-leafed bush or
tree does not exist.   The best shade to be found
on the desert is under the mesquite, and unless
it is very large, the sun falls through it easily
enough.

* I am indebted to Professor Forbes of the University
of Arizona for this and several other statements in connection with desert vegetation.

As an extra precaution some shrubs are given a shellac-like sap or gum with which they varnish their leaves and make evaporation almost impossible. The ordinary greasewood is an example of this ; and perhaps because of its varnish, it is, with the cacti, the hardiest of all the desert growths. It is found wherever anything living is found, and flourishes under the fiercest heat. Its leaves always look bright and have a sticky feeling about them as though recently shellacked.

Gums and varnishes of bushes.

There are other growths that seem to have a fine sense of discretion in the matter of danger, for they let fall all their leaves at the first approach of drouth. The ocatilla, or "candle wood " as it is sometimes called, puts out a long row of bright leaves along its stems after a rain, but as soon as drouth comes it sheds them hastily and then stands for months in the sunlight —a bundle of bare sticks soaked with a resin that will burn with fire, but will not evaporate with heat. The sangre de dragon (sometimes called sangre en grado) does the same thing.

The ocatilla.

But Nature's most common device for the protection and preservation of her desert brood is to supply them with wonderful facilities for finding and sapping what moisture there is, and

Tap roots.

conserving it in tanks and reservoirs. The roots of the greasewood and the mesquite are almost as powerful as the arms of an octopus, and they are frequently three times the length of the bush or tree they support. They will bore their way through rotten granite to find a damp ledge almost as easily as a diamond drill; and they will pry rocks from their foundations as readily as the wistaria wrenches the ornamental wood-work from the roof of a porch. They are always thirsty and they are always running

Under-
ground
structure.

here and there in the search for moisture. A vertical section of their underground structure revealed by the cutting away of a river bank or wash is usually a great surprise. One marvels at the great network of roots required to support such a very little growth above ground.

Yet this network serves a double purpose. It not only finds and gathers what moisture there is but stores it in its roots, feeding the

Feeding the
top growth.

top growth with it economically, not wastefully. It has no notion of sending too much moisture up to the sunlight and the air. Cut a twig and it will often appear very dry; cut a root and you will find it moist.

The storage reservoir below ground is not an unusual method of supplying water to the plant.

Many of the desert growths have it. Perhaps the most notable example of it is the wild gourd. This is little more than an enormous tap root that spreads out turnip-shaped and is in size often as large around as a man's body. It holds water in its pulpy tissue for months at a time, and while almost everything above ground is parched and dying the vines and leaves of the gourd, fed from the reservoir below, will go on growing and the flowers continue blooming with the most unruffled serenity. In the Sonora deserts there is a cactus or a bush (its name I have never heard) growing from a root that looks almost like a hornet's nest. This root is half-wood, half-vegetable, and is again a water reservoir like the root of the gourd.

Storage reservoirs below ground.

But there are reservoirs above ground quite as interesting as those below. The tall fluted column of the sahuaro, sometimes fifty feet high, is little more than an upright cistern for holding moisture. Its support within is a series of sticks arranged in cylindrical form and held together by some fibre, some tissue, and a great deal of saturated pulp. Drive a stick into it after a rain and it will run sap almost like the maguey from which the Indians distill mescal. All the cacti conserve water in their

Reservoirs above ground.

lobes or columns or at the base near the ground. So too the Spanish bayonets, the yuccas, the prickly pears and the chollas.

Many of the shrubs and trees like the sangre de dragon and the torote have enlarged or thickened barks to hold and supply water. If you cut them the sap runs readily. When it

Thickened barks.

congeals it forms a gum which heals over the wound and once more prevents evaporation. Existence for the plants would be impossible without such inventions. Plant life of every kind requires some moisture all the time. It is an error to suppose because they grow in the so-called " rainless desert " that therefore they exist without water. They gather and husband it during wet periods for use during dry

Gathering moisture.

periods, and in doing so they seem to display almost as much intelligence as a squirrel or an ant does in storing food for winter consumption.

Is Nature's task completed then when she has provided the plants with reservoirs of water and tap roots to pump for them ? By no means. How long would a tank of moisture exist in the

Attacks upon desert plants.

desert if unprotected from the desert animals ? The mule-deer lives here, and he can go for weeks without water, but he will take it every day if he can get it. And the coyote can run the hills indefinitely with little or no moisture; but he will eat a water melon, rind and all, and with great relish, when the opportunity offers. The sahuaro, the bisnaga, the cholla, and the pan-cake lobed prickly pear would have a short life and not a merry one if they were left to the mercy of the desert prowler. As it is they are sometimes sadly worried about their roots by rabbits and in their lobes by the deer. It seems almost incredible but is not the less a fact, that deer and desert cattle will eat the cholla—fruit, stem, and trunk—though it bristles with spines that will draw blood from the human hand at the slightest touch.

Browsing animals.

Nature knows very well that the attack will come and so she provides her plants with various different defenses. The most common weapon which she gives them is the spine or thorn. Almost everything that grows has it and its different forms are many. They are all of them sharp as a needle and some of them have saw-edges that rip anything with which they come in contact. The grasses, and those plants akin to them like the yucca and the maguey, are often both saw-edged and spine-pointed. All the cacti have thorns, some straight, some barbed like a harpoon, some curved like a hook.

Weapons of defense.

There are chollas that have a sheath covering the thorn—a scabbard to the sword—and when anything pushes against it the sheath is left sticking in the wound. The different forms of the bisnaga are little more than vegetable porcupines. They bristle with quills or have hook-shaped thorns that catch and hold the intruder. *The spine and thorn,* The sahuaro has not so many spines, but they are so arranged that you can hardly strike the cylinder without striking the thorns.

The cacti are defended better than the other growths because they have more to lose, and are consequently more subject to attack. And yet there is one notable exception. The crucifixion thorn is a bush or tree somewhat like the palo verde, except that it has no leaf. It is a *The cruci-fixion thorn.* thorn and little else. Each small twig runs out and ends in a sharp spike of which the branch is but the supporting shaft. It bears in August a small yellow flower but this grows out of the side of the spike. In fact the whole shrub seems created for no other purpose than the glorification of the thorn as a thorn.*

* It is said to be very scarce but I have found it growing along the Castle Creek region of Arizona, also at Kingman, Peach Springs, and further north. A stunted variety grows on the Mojave but it is not frequently seen on the Colorado.

Tree, bush, plant and grass—great and small alike—each has its sting for the intruder. You can hardly stoop to pick a desert flower or pull a bunch of small grass without being aware of a prickle on your hand. Nature seems to have provided a whole arsenal of defensive weapons for these poor starved plants of the desert. Not any of the lovely growths of the earth, like the lilies and the daffodils, are so well defended. And she has given them not only armor but a spirit of tenacity and stubbornness wherewith to carry on the struggle. Cut out the purslain and the iron weed from the garden walk, and it springs up again and again, contending for life. Put heat, drouth, and animal attack against the desert shrubs and they fight back like the higher forms of organic life. How typical they are of everything in and about the desert. There is but one word to describe it and that word—fierce—I shall have worn threadbare before I have finished these chapters.

The sting of flowers.

Fierceness of the plant.

We have not yet done with enumerating the defenses of these plants. The bushes like the greasewood and the sage have not the bulk of body to grow the thorn. They are too slight, too rambling in make-up. Besides their reservoirs are protected by being in their roots under

Odors and juices.

the ground. But Nature has not left their tops wholly at the mercy of the deer. Take the leaf of the sage and crush it in your hand. The odor is anything but pleasant. No animal except the jack-rabbit, no bird except the sage hen will eat it; and no human being will eat either the rabbit or the hen, if he can get anything else, because of the rank sage flavor. Rub the greasewood in your hand and it feels harsh and brittle. The resinous varnish of the leaves gives it a sticky feeling and a disagreeable odor again. Nothing on the desert will touch

Saps astringent and cathartic.

it. Cut or break a twig of the sangre de dragon and a red sap like blood runs out. Touch it to the tongue and it proves the most powerful of astringents. The Indians use it to cauterize bullet wounds. Again no animal will touch it. Half the plants on the desert put forth their leaves with impunity. They are not disturbed by either browsers or grazers. Some of them are poisonous, many of them are cathartic or emetic, nearly all of them are disagreeable to the taste.

So it seems with spines, thorns, barbs, resins, varnishes and odorous smells Nature has armed her desert own very effectually. And her expenditure of energy may seem singularly dis-

proportionate to the result attained.   The little *The expend-iture of energy.*
vegetation that grows in the waste may not
seem worth while, may seem insignificant
compared with the great care bestowed upon it.
But Nature does not think so. To her the cactus of the desert is just as important in its
place as the arrowy pine on the mountain.
She means that something shall grow and bear
fruit after its kind even on the gravel beds of
the Colorado ; she means that the desert shall
have its covering, scanty though it be, just the *The desert covering.*
same as the well-watered lands of the tropics.

But are they useful, these desert growths ?
Certainly they are ; just as useful as the pine
tree or the potato plant. To be sure, man
cannot saw them into boards or cook them in a
pot ; but then Nature has other animals be-
side man to look after, other uses for her pro- *Use of desert plants.*
ducts than supporting human life. She toils
and spins for all alike and man is not her special care. The desert vegetation answers her
purposes and who shall say her purposes have
ever been other than wise ?

Are they beautiful these plants and shrubs
of the desert ? Now just what do you mean
by that word "beautiful" ? Do you mean
something of regular form, something smooth

and pretty? Are you dragging into nature some remembrances of classic art; and are you looking for the Dionysius face, the Doryphorus form, among these trees and bushes? If so the desert will not furnish you too much of beauty. But if you mean something that has a distinct character, something appropriate to its setting, something admirably fitted to a designed end (as in art the peasants of Millet or the burghers of Rembrandt and Rodin), then the desert will show forth much that people nowadays are beginning to think beautiful. Mind you, perfect form and perfect

color are not to be despised; neither shall you despise perfect fitness and perfect character. The desert plants, every one of them, have very positive characters; and I am not certain but that many of them are interesting and beautiful even in form and color.

No doubt it is an acquired taste that leads one to admire greasewood and cactus; but can anyone be blind to the graceful form of the maguey, or better still, the yucca with its tall stalk rising like a shaft from a bowl and capped

at the top by nodding creamy flowers? On the mountains and the mesas the sahuaro is so common that perhaps we overlook its beauty of form ; yet its lines are as sinuous as those of a Moslem minaret, its flutings as perfect as those of a Doric column. Often and often you see it standing on a ledge of some rocky peak, like the lone shaft of a ruined temple on a Greek headland. And by way of contrast what could be more lovely than the waving lightness, the drooping gracefulness of the lluvia d'oro. The *The lluvia d'oro.* swaying tossing lluvia d'oro, well called the " shower of gold " ! It is one of the most beautiful of the desert trees with its white skin like the northern birch, its long needles like the pine, and the downward sweep of its branches like the willow. A strange wild tree that seems to shun all society, preferring to dwell like a hermit among the rocks. It roots itself in the fissures of broken granite and it seems at its happiest when it can let down its shower of gold over some precipice.

There are other tree forms, like the palo verde and the mesquite, that are not wanting in a native grace ; and yet it may as well be admitted that most of the trees and bushes are lacking in height, mass, and majesty. It is no place *Grotesque forms.* for large growths that reach up to the sun. The heat and drouth are too great and tend to make form angular and grotesque. But these very conditions that dwarf form perhaps enhance color by distorting it in an analogous manner. When plants are starved for water and grow in thin poor soil they often put on colors that are abnormal, even unhealthy. Because of starvation perhaps the little green of the desert is a sallow green ; and for the same reason the lobes of the prickly pear are pale-green, dull yellow, sad pink or livid mauve. The prickly pear seems to take all colors dependent upon the poverty, or the mineral character, of the ground where it grows. In that respect perhaps it is influenced in the same way as the parti-colored hydrangea of the eastern dooryard.

Abnormal colors.

All the cacti are brilliant in the flowers they bear. The top of the bisnaga in summer is at first a mass of yellow, then bright orange, finally dark red. The sahuaro bears a purple flower, and the cholla, the ocatilla, the pitahaya come along with pink or gold or red or blue flowers. And again all the bushes and trees in summer put forth showers of color—graceful masses of petaled cups that look more like flowers grown in a meadow than blossoms grown on a tree. In June the palo verde is a great ball of yellow-gold, but there is a variety of it with a blue-green bark that grows a blossom almost like an

Blossoms and flowers.

eastern violet. And down in Sonora one is dazzled by the splendor of the guyacan (or guallacan) which throws out blossoms half-blue and half-red. All the commoner growths like the sage, the mesquite, the palo fierro, and the palo blanco, are blossom bearers. In fact everything that grows at all in the desert puts forth in season some bright little flag of color. In the mass they make little show, but examined in the part they are interesting because of their nurture, their isolation, and their peculiarity of form and color. The conditions of life have perhaps contorted them, have paled or grayed or flushed or made morbid their coloring; but they are all of them beautiful. Beautiful color is usually unhealthy color as we have already suggested.

Many varieties.

Aside from the blossoms upon bush and tree there are few bright petals shining in the desert. It is no place for flowers. They are too delicate and are usually wanting in tap root and armor. If they spring up they are soon cut down by drouth or destroyed by animals. Many tales are told of the flowers that grow on the waste after the rains, but I have not seen them though I have seen the rains. There are no lupins, phacelias, pentstemons, poppies, or

Wild flowers.

yellow violets. Occasionally one sees the wild
verbena or patches of the evening primrose, or
up in the swales the little baby blue-eye growing all alone, or perhaps the yellow mimulus;
but all told they do not make up a very strong
Salt-bush. contingent. The salt bush that looks the color
of Scotch heather, out-bulks them all; and yet
is not conspicuously apparent. Higher up in the
hills and along the mesas one often meets with
many strange flowers, some fiery red and some
with spines like the Canadian thistle; but not
down in the hot valleys of the desert.

The grasses. Nor are there many grasses of consequence
aside from a small curled grass and the heavy
sacaton that grow in bunches upon isolated
portions of the desert. By "isolated" I mean
that for some unknown reason there are tracts
on the desert seemingly sacred to certain plants,
some to cholla, some to yuccas, some to grease
wood, some to sahuaros, some to sacaton grass.
It seems to be a desert oddity that the vegetation does not mix or mingle to any great extent. There are seldom more than four or five
kinds of growth to be found in one tract. It
The lichens. is even noticeable in the lichens. One mountain range will have all gray lichens on its
northern walls, another range will have all

orange lichens, and still another will be mottled by patches of coal-black lichens.

Strange growths of a strange land! Heat, drouth, and starvation gnawing at their vitals month in and month out; and yet how determined to live, how determined to fulfill their destiny! They keep fighting off the elements, the animals, the birds. Never by day or by night do they loose the armor or drop the spear point. And yet with all the struggle they serenely blossom in season, perpetuate their kinds, and hand down the struggle to the newer generation with no jot of vigor abated, no tittle of hope dissipated. Strange growths indeed! And yet strange, perhaps, only to us who have never known their untrumpeted history.

The continuous struggle.

CHAPTER IX

DESERT ANIMALS

THE life of the desert lives only by virtue of adapting itself to the conditions of the desert. Nature does not bend the elements to favor the plants and the animals; she makes the plants and the animals do the bending. The torote *Meeting desert requirements.* and the evening primrose must get used to heat, drouth, and a rocky bed; the coyote must learn to go without food and water for long periods. Even man, whose magnificent complacency leads him to think himself one of Nature's favorites, fares no better than a wild cat or an angle of cholla. He must endure the same heat, thirst, and hunger or perish. There is no other alternative.

And so it happens that those things that can live in the desert become stamped after a time with a peculiar desert character. The struggle *The peculiar desert character.* seems to develop in them special characteristics and make them, not different from their kind; but more positive, more insistent. The yucca

150

of the Mojave is the yucca of New Mexico and
Old Mexico but hardier; the wild cat of the
Colorado is the wild cat of Virginia but swifter,
more ferocious; the Yuma Indian is like the
Zuni or the Navajo but lanker, more sinewy,
more enduring. Father Garces, who passed
through here one hundred and twenty-five years
ago, records in his *Memoirs* more than once the
wonderful endurance of the desert Indians.
"The Jamajabs (a branch of the Yumas) endure hunger and thirst for four days," he writes
in one place. The tale is told that the Indians *Desert
Indians.*
in the Coahuila Valley at the present day can
do substantially the same thing. And, too, it
is said that the Yumas have traveled from the
Colorado to the Pacific, across the desert on
foot, without any sustenance whatever. No
one, not to the desert born, could do such a
thing. Years of training in starvation, thirst
and exposure have produced a man almost as
hardy as the cactus, and just as distinctly a
type of the desert as the coyote.

But the Indian and the plant must have *some*
water. They cannot go without it indefinitely.
And just there the desert animals seem to fit *The
animals.*
their environment a little snugger than either
plant or human. For, strange as it may ap-

pear, many of them get no water at all. There are sections of the desert, fifty or more miles square, where there is not a trace of water in river, creek, arroyo or pocket, where there is never a drop of dew falling; and where the two or three showers of rain each year sink into the sand and are lost in half an hour after they have fallen. Yet that fifty-mile tract of sand and rock supports its animal, reptile and insect life just the same as a similar tract in Illinois or Florida. How the animals endure, how—even on the theory of getting used to it—the jack-rabbit, the ground squirrel, the rat, and the gopher can live for months without even the moisture from green vegetation, is one of the mysteries. A mirror held to the nose of a desert rabbit will show a moist breath-mark on the glass. The moisture came out of the rabbit, is coming out of him every few seconds of the day; and there is not a drop of moisture going into him. Evidently the ancient axiom: "Out of nothing, nothing comes" is all wrong.

Life without water.

It is said in answer that the jack-rabbit gets moisture from roots, cactus-lobes and the like. And the reply is that you find him where there are no roots but greasewood and no cactus at

Endurance of the jack-rabbit.

all. Besides there is no evidence from an examination of his stomach that he ever eats anything but dried grass, bark, and sage leaves. But if the matter is a trifle doubtful about the rabbit on account of his traveling capacities, there is no doubt whatever about the ground squirrels, the rock squirrels, and the prairie dogs. None of them ever gets more than a hundred yards from his hole in his life, except possibly when migrating. And the circuit about each hole is usually bare of everything except dried grass. There in no moisture to be had. The prairie dog is not found on the desert, but in Wyoming and Montana there are villages of them on the grass prairies, with no water, root, lobe, or leaf within miles of them. The old theory of the prairie dog digging his hole down to water has no basis in fact. Patience, a strong arm and a spade will get to the bottom of his burrow in half an hour.

Rock squirrels.

Prairie dogs and water.

All the desert animals know the meaning of a water famine, and even those that are pronounced water drinkers know how to get on with the minimum supply. The mule-deer whose cousin in the Adirondacks goes down to water every night, lives in the desert mountains, month in and month out with nothing more

Water famine.

watery to quench thirst than a lobe of the
prickly pear or a joint of cholla. But he is naturally fond of green vegetation, and in the early
morning he usually leaves the valley and climbs
the mountains where with goats and mountain

Mule-deer browsing.

sheep he browses on the twigs of shrub and tree.
The coyote likes water, too, but he puts up with
sucking a nest of quail eggs, eating some mesquite beans, or at best absorbing the blood from
some rabbit. The wild cat will go for weeks
without more moisture than the blood of birds
or lizards, and then perhaps, after long thirst,
he will come to a water pocket in the rocks to
lap only a handful, doing it with an angry

Coyotes and wild-cats living without water.

snarling snap as though he disliked it and was
drinking under compulsion. The gray wolf
is too much of a traveler to depend upon any
one locality. He will run fifty miles in a night
and be back before morning. Whether he
gets water or not is not possible to ascertain.
The badger, the coon, and the bear are very
seldom seen in the more arid regions. They
are not strictly speaking desert animals because
unfitted to endure desert hardships. They are
naturally great eaters and sleepers, loving cool
weather and their own fatness; and to that the
desert is sharply opposed. There is nothing

fat in the land of sand and cactus. Animal
life is lean and gaunt; if it sleeps at all it is with
one eye open ; and as for heat it cares very little about it. For the first law of the desert to
which animal life of every kind pays allegiance
is the law of endurance and abstinence. After
that requirement is fulfilled special needs produce the peculiar qualities and habits of the individual.

Lean,
gaunt life.

Yet there is one quality more general than
special since almost everything possesses it, and
that is ferocity—fierceness. The strife is desperate ; the supply of food and moisture is
small, the animal is very hungry and thirsty.
What wonder then that there is the determi-
nation of the starving in all desert life ! Everything pursues or is pursued. Every muscle is
strung to the highest tension. The bounding
deer must get away; the swift-following wolf
must not let him. The gray lizard dashes for
a ledge of rock like a flash of light ; but the
bayonet bill of the road runner must catch
him before he gets there. Neither can afford
to miss his mark. And that is perhaps the
reason why there is so much development in
special directions, so much fitness for a particular purpose, so much equipment for the

Fierceness
of the
animals.

Fitness for
attack and
escape.

doing or the avoiding of death. Because the wild-cat cannot afford to miss his quarry, therefore is he made a something that seldom does miss.

The wild-
cat.

The description of the lion as "a jaw on four paws" will fit the wild-cat very well—only he is a jaw on two paws. The hind legs are insignificant compared with the front ones, and the body back of the shoulders is lean, lank, slight, but withal muscular and sinewy. The head is bushy, heavy, and square, the neck and shoulders are massive, the forelegs and paws so large that they look to belong to some other animal. The ears are small yet sensitive enough to catch the least noise, the nose is acute, the eyes are like great mirrors, the teeth like points of steel. In fact the whole animal is little more than a machine for dragging down and devouring prey. That and the protection of his breed are his only missions on earth. He is the same creeping, snarling beast that one finds in the mountains of California, but the desert animal is larger and stronger. He sneaks upon a band of quail or a rabbit with greater caution, and

The spring
of the cat.

when he springs and strikes it is with greater certainty. The enormous paws pin the game to the earth, and the sharp teeth cut through like knives. It is not more than once in two or three days that a meal comes within reach and he has no notion of allowing it to get away.

The panther, or as he is more commonly called, the mountain lion, is no such square-built mass of muscle, no such bundle of energy as the wild-cat, though much longer and larger. The figure is wiry and serpentine, and has all the action and grace of the tiger. It is pre-eminently a figure for crouching, sneaking, springing, and dragging down. His struggle-for-life is perhaps not so desperate as that of the cat because he lives high up in the desert mountains where game is more plentiful ; but he is a very good struggler for all that. Occasionally one hears his cry in the night (a cry that stops the yelp of the coyote very quickly and sets the ears of the jack-rabbit a-trembling) but he is seldom seen unless sought for. Even then the seeker does not usually care to look for him, or at him too long. He has the tiger eye, and his jaw and claw are too powerful to be trifled with. He will not attack one unless at bay or wounded ; but as a mountain prowler he is the terror of the young deer, the mountain sheep, and the rabbit family.

One sees the gray wolf but little oftener than the mountain lion. Sometimes in the very

The mountain lion.

Habits of the mountain lion.

The gray wolf.

early morning you may catch a glimpse of him
sneaking up a mountain canyon, but he usually
keeps out of sight. His size is great for a wolf
—sometimes over six feet from nose to tail tip
—but it lies mostly in length and bulk. He does
not stand high on his feet and yet is a swift and
long-winded runner. In this and in his strength
of jaw lies his special equipment. He is not
very cunning but he takes up and follows a
trail, and runs the game to earth with considerable perseverance. I have never seen anything
but his footprints on the desert. Usually he
keeps well up in the mountains and comes down
on the plains only at night. He prefers prairie
or table-land country, with adjacent stock
Home of the wolf. ranges, to the desert, because there the hunting
is not difficult. Sheep, calves, and pigs he will
eat with some relish, but his favorite game is the
young colt. He runs all his game and catches
it as it runs like the true wolf that he is. Sometimes he hunts in packs of half a dozen, but if
there is no companionship he does not hesitate
to hunt alone.

The coyote. The prairie wolf or coyote is not at all like
the gray wolf. He seldom runs after things,
though he does a good deal of running away
from them. And he is a fairly good runner too.

But he does not win his living by his courage. His special gift is not the muscular energy that crushes at a blow ; nor the great strength that follows and tires and finally drags down. Nature designed him with the wolf form and instinct, but gave him something of the cleverness of the fox. It is by cunning and an obliging stomach that the coyote is enabled to eke out a living. He is cunning enough to know, for instance, that you cannot see him on a desert background as long as he does not move ; so he sits still at times for many minutes, watching you from some little knoll. As long as he is motionless your eyes pass over him as a patch of sand or a weathered rock. When he starts to move, it is with some deliberation. He prefers a dog-trot and often several shots from your rifle will not stir him into a run. He slips along easily and gracefully—a lean, hungry-looking wretch with all the insolence of a hoodlum and all the shrewdness of a thief. He requires just such qualities together with a keen nose, good eyes and ears, and some swiftness of dash to make a living. The desert bill of fare is not all that a wolf could desire ; but the coyote is not very particular. Everything is food that comes to his jaws. He likes rabbit meat, but

Cleverness of the coyote.

does not often get it. For desert rabbits do not go to sleep with both eyes shut. Failing the rabbit he snuffs out birds and their nests, *His subsistence.* trails up anything sick or wounded, and in emergencies runs down and devours a lizard. If animal food is scarce he turns his attention to vegetation, eats prickly pears and mesquite beans; and up in the mountains he stands on his hind legs and gathers choke cherries and manzanitas. With such precarious living he becomes gaunt, leathery, muscled with whip-cord. There is a meagreness and a scantiness about him; his coarse coat of hair is sun-scorched, his whole appearance is arid, dusty, sandy. There is no other animal so thoroughly typical of the desert. *His background.* He belongs there, skulking along the arroyos and washes just as a horned toad belongs under a granite bowlder. That he can live there at all is due to Nature's gift to him of all-around cleverness.

The fox The fox is usually accounted the epitome of animal cunning, but here in the desert he is not frequently seen and is usually thought less clever than the coyote. He prefers the foothills and the cover of dense chaparral where he preys upon birds, smells out the nest of the valley quail, catches a wood-rat; or, if hard

pushed to it, makes a meal of crickets and grass-
hoppers.   But even at this he is not more facile
than the coyote.   Nor can he surpass the coyote
in robbing a hen-roost and keeping out of a
trap while doing it.   He cuts no important figure on the desert and, indeed, he is hardly a
desert animal though sometimes found there.
The conditions of existence are too severe for
him.   The strength of the cat, the legs of the
wolf, and the stomach of the coyote are not his;
and so he prowls nearer civilization and takes
more risk for an easier life.

And the prey, what of the prey!   The ani- *The prey.*
mals of the desert that furnish food for the
meat eaters like the wolf and the cat—the animals that cannot fight back or at least wage unequal warfare—are they left hopelessly and help-
lessly at the mercy of the destroyers?   Not so.
Nature endows them and protects them as best
she can.   Every one of them has some device to
baffle or trick the enemy.   Even the poor little
horned toad, that has only his not too thick
skin to save him, can slightly change the color
of that skin to suit the bowlder he is flattened   *Devices for*
upon so that the keenest eye would pass him   *escape.*
over unnoticed.   The jack-rabbit cannot change
his skin, but he knows many devices whereby he

contrives to save it. Lying in his form at the root of some bush or cactus he is not easily seen. He crouches low and the gray of his fur fits into the sand imperceptibly. You do not see him but he sees you. His eyes never close; *Senses of the rabbit.* they are always watching. Look at them closely as he lies dead before you and how large and protruding they are ! In the life they see everything that moves. And if his eyes fail him, perhaps his ears will not. He was named the jackass-rabbit because of his long ears ; and the length of them is in exact proportion to their acuteness of hearing. No footstep escapes them. They are natural megaphones for the reception of sound. It can hardly be doubted that his nose is just as acute as his eyes and his ears. So that all told he is not an animal easily caught napping.

And if the jack-rabbit's senses fail him, has he no other resource ? Certainly, yes ; that is if he is not captured. In proportion to his size he has the strongest hind legs of anything on *Speed of the jack-rabbit.* the desert. In this respect he is almost like a kangaroo. When he starts running and begins with his long bound, there is nothing that can overtake him except a trained greyhound. He ricochets from knoll to knoll like a bounding ball, and as he crosses ahead of you perhaps you think he is not moving very fast. But shoot at him and see how far behind him your rifle ball strikes the dust. No coyote or wolf is foolish enough to chase him or ever try to run him down. His endurance is quite as good as his speed. It makes no difference about his not drinking water and that all his energy comes from bark and dry grass. He keeps right on running; over stones, through cactus, down a canyon, up a mountain. For keen senses and swift legs he is the desert type as emphatically as the coyote that is forever prowling on his track.

His endurance.

The little " cotton-tail " rabbit is not perhaps so well provided for as the jack-rabbit; but then he does not live in the open and is not so exposed to attack. He hides in brush, weeds, or grass; and when startled makes a quick dash for a hole in the ground or a ledge of rock. His legs are good for a short distance, and his senses are acute; but the wild-cat or the coyote catches him at last. The continuance of his species lies in prolific breeding. The wild-cat, too, catches a good many gophers, rats, mice, and squirrels. The squirrels are many in kind and beautiful in their forms and colorings. One

The "cotton-tail."

can hardly count them all—squirrels with long tails and short tails and no tails ; squirrels yellow, brown, gray, blue, and slate-colored. They live in the rocks about the bases of the desert mountains ; and eventually they fall a prey to the wild-cat who watches for them just as the domestic cat watches for the house rat. Their only safeguard is their energetic way of darting into a hole. For all their sharp noses and ears they are foolish little folk and will keep poking their heads out to see what is going on.

Squirrels and gophers.

But for acute senses, swift legs, and powerful endurance nothing can surpass the antelope. He is rarely seen to-day (more's the pity !) ; but only a few years ago there were quite a number of them on the Sonora edge of the Colorado Desert. Usually they prefer the higher mesas where the land is grass-grown and the view is unobstructed ; but they have been known to come far down into the desert. And the antelope is very well fitted for the sandy waste. The lack of water does not bother him, he can eat anything that grows in grass or bush ; and he can keep from being eaten about as cleverly as any of the deer tribe. His eye alone is a marvel of development. It protrudes from the socket

The desert antelope.

His eyes.

—bulges out almost like the end of an egg—
and if there were corners on the desert mesas
I believe that eye could see around them. He
cannot be approached in any direction without
seeing what is going on; but he may be still-
hunted and shot from behind crag or cover.

His curiosity is usually the death of him, because he will persist in standing still and looking at things; but his senses almost always give
him fair warning. His nose and ears are just *His nose and ears.*
as acute as his eyes. And how he can run!
His legs seem to open and shut like the blades
of a pocket-knife, so leisurely, so apparently
effortless. But how they do take him over the
ground! With one leg shot from under him
he runs pretty nearly as fast as before. A
tougher, more wiry, more beautiful animal was
never created. Perhaps that is the reason why
every man's hand has been raised against him
until now his breed is almost extinct. He was
well fitted to survive on the desert mesas and
the upland plains—a fine type of swiftness and *His swiftness.*
endurance—but Nature in her economy never
reckoned with the magazine rifle nor the greed
of the individual who calls himself a sports-
man.

The mule-deer with his large ears, long muz-

zle and keen eyes, is almost as well provided for
as the antelope. He has survived the antelope
possibly because he does not live in the open
country. He haunts the brush and the rock
cover of the gorge and the mountain side.
There in the heavy chaparral he will skulk
and hide while you may pass within a few feet
of him. If he sees that he is discovered he
can make a dash up or down the mountain in
a way that astonishes. Stones, sticks, and brush
have no terror for him. He jumps over them
or smashes through them. He will bound
across a talus of broken porphyry that will cut
the toughest boots to pieces, striking all four
feet with every bound, and yet not ruffle the
hair around his dew claws; or he will dash
through a tough dry chaparral at full speed
without receiving a scrape or a cut of any kind.

The speed he attains on such ground astonishes again. His feet seem to strike rubber instead of stone; for he bounds like a ball, describes a quarter circle, and bounds again. The
magazine of your rifle may be emptied at him;
and still he may go on, gayly cutting quarter
circles, until he disappears over the ridge. He
is one of the hardiest of the desert progeny.
The lack of water affects him little. He browses

and gets fat on twigs and leaves that seem to have as little nutriment about them as a telegraph-pole ; and he lies down on a bed of stones as upon a bed of roses. He is as tough as the goats and sheep that keep well up on the high mountain ridges ; and in cleverness is perhaps superior to the antelope. But oftentimes he will turn around to have a last look, and therein lies his undoing. In Sonora there is found a dwarf deer—a foolish if pretty little creature—and along river-beds the white-tailed deer is occasionally seen ; but these deer with the goats and the sheep hardly belong to the desert, though living upon its confines.

Habits of the desert-deer.

The white-tail.

In fact, none of the far-travelling animals lives right down in the desert gravel-beds continuously. They go there at night or in the early morning, but in the daytime they are usually found in the neighboring hills. The rabbits, rats, and squirrels, if undisturbed, will usually stay upon the flat ground ; and there is also another variety of desert life that does not wander far from the sand and the rocks. I mean the reptiles. They are not as a class swift in flight, nor over-clever in sense, nor cunning in devices. Nor have they sufficient strength to grapple and fight with the larger animals. It

The reptiles.

would seem as though Nature had brought them into the desert only half made-up—a prey to every beast and bird. But no; they are given the most deadly weapon of defence of all

Poison of reptiles.

—poison. Almost all of the reptiles have poison about them in fang or sting. We are accustomed to label them " poisonous " or "not poisonous," as they kill or do not kill a human being; but that is not the proper criterion by which to judge. The bite of the trap-door spider will not seriously affect a man, but it will kill a lizard in a few minutes. In proportion to his size the common red ant of the desert is more poisonous than the rattlesnake. It is reiterated with much positiveness that a swarm of these ants have been known to kill men. There is, however, only one reptile on the

The fang and sting.

desert that humanity need greatly fear on account of his poison and that is the rattlesnake. There are several varieties called in local parlance " side-winders," " ground rattlers," and the like; but the ordinary spotted, brown, or yellow rattlesnake is the type. He is not a pleasant creature, but then he is not often met with. In travelling many hundreds of miles on the desert I never encountered more than half a dozen.

The rattle is indescribable, but a person will know it the first time he hears it. It is something between a buzz and a burr, and can cause a cold perspiration in a minute fraction of time. The snake is very slow in getting ready to strike, in fact sluggish; but once the head shoots out, it does so with the swiftness of an arrow. Nothing except the road-runner can dodge it. The poison is deadly if the fang has entered a vein or a fleshy portion of the body where the flow of blood to the heart is free. If struck on the hand or foot, the man may recover, because the circulation there is slow and the heart has time to repel the attack. Every animal on the desert knows just how venomous is that poison. Even your dog knows it by instinct. He may shake and kill garter-snakes, but he will not touch the rattlesnake.

The rattle-snake.

Effect of the poison.

All of the spider family are poisonous and you can find almost every one of them on the desert. The most sharp-witted of the family is the trap-door spider—the name coming from the door which he hinges and fastens over the entrance of his hole in the ground. The tarantula is simply an overgrown spider, very heavy in weight, and inclined to be slow and stupid in action. He is a ferocious-looking wretch

Spiders and tarantulas.

and has a ferocious bite. It makes an ugly
wound and is deadly enough to small animals.
The scorpion has the reputation of being very
venomous; but his sting on the hand amounts
to little more than that of an ordinary wasp.

Nor is the long-bodied, many-legged, rather
graceful centipede so great a poison-carrier as
has been alleged. They are all of them poisonous, but in varying degrees. Doubtless the
(to us) harmless horned toads and the swifts
have for their enemies some venom in store.

The lizards are many in variety, and their
colors are often very beautiful in grays, yellows,
reds, blues, and indigoes. The Gila monster
belongs to their family, though he is much
larger. The look of him is very forbidding and
he has an ugly way of hissing at you; but just
how venomous he is I do not know. Very
likely there is some poison about him, though
this has been denied. It would seem that everything that cannot stand or run or hide must
be defended somehow. Even the poor little

skunk when he comes to live on the desert develops poisoned teeth and his bite produces
what is called hydrophobia. The truth about
the hydrophobia skunk is, I imagine, that he is
an eater of carrion; and when he bites a per-

son he is likely to produce blood-poisoning, which is miscalled hydrophobia.

Taking them for all in all, they seem like a precious pack of cutthroats, these beasts and reptiles of the desert. Perhaps there never was a life so nurtured in violence, so tutored in attack and defence as this. The warfare is continuous from the birth to the death. Everything must fight, fly, feint, or use poison ; and every slayer eventually becomes a victim. What a murderous brood for Nature to bring forth ! And what a place she has chosen in which to breed them ! Not only the struggle among themselves, but the struggle with the land, the elements — the eternal fighting with heat, drouth, and famine. What else but fierceness and savagery could come out of such conditions ?

The cutthroat band.

The eternal struggle.

But, after all, is there not something in the sheer brute courage that endures, worthy of our admiration ? These animals have made the best out of the worst, and their struggle has given them a physical character which is, shall we not say, beautiful ? Perhaps you shudder at the thought of a panther dragging down a deer— one enormous paw over the deer's muzzle, one on his neck, and the strain of all the back mus-

Brute courage.

cles coming into play. But was not that the
purpose for which the panther was designed ?
As a living machine how wonderfully he works!
Look at the same subject done in bronze by
Barye and you will see what a revelation of
Brute character. character the great statuary thought it. Look,
too, at Barye's wolf and fox, look at the lions of
Géricault, and the tigers and serpents of Dela-
croix ; and with all the jaw and poison of them
how beautiful they are !

You will say they are made beautiful through
the art of the artists, and that is partly true ;
but we are seeing only what the artists saw.
And how did they come to choose such sub-
jects ? Why, simply because they recognized
that for art there is no such thing as nobility or
vulgarity of subject. Everything may be fit if
Beauty in character. it possesses character. The beautiful is the
characteristic—the large, full-bodied, well-ex-
pressed truth of character. At least that is one
very positive phase of beauty.

Even the classic idea of beauty, which re-
Graceful forms of animals. gards only the graceful in form or movement
or the sensuous in color, finds types among
these desert inhabitants. The dullest person
in the arts could not but see fine form and proportion in the panther, graceful movement in

the antelope, and charm of color in all the pretty rock squirrels. For myself, being somewhat prejudiced in favor of this drear waste and its savage progeny, I may confess to having watched the flowing movements of snakes, their coil and rattle and strike, many times and with great pleasure; to having stretched myself for hours upon granite bowlders while following the play of indigo lizards in the sand; to having traced with surprise the slightly changing skin of the horned toad produced by the reflection of different colors held near him.

Colors of lizards.

I may also confess that common as is the jack-rabbit he never bursts away in speed before me without being followed by my wonder at his graceful mystery of motion; that the crawl of a wild-cat upon game is something that arrests and fascinates by its masterful skill; and that even that desert tramp, the coyote, is entitled to admiration for the graceful way he can slip through patches of cactus. The fault is not in the subject. It is not vulgar or ugly. The trouble is that we perhaps have not the proper angle of vision. If we understood all, we should admire all.

Mystery of motion.

CHAPTER X

WINGED LIFE

THE desert's secrets of life and growth and death are not to be read at a glance. The first day's walk is usually a disappointment. You see little more than a desolate waste. The light of the blue sky, the subtle color of the air, the roll of the valleys, the heave of the mountains do not reveal themselves at once. The vegetation you think looks like a thin covering of dry sticks. And as for the animals, the birds —the living things on the desert—they are not apparent at all.

The first day's walk.

But the casual stroll does not bring you to the end of the desert's resources. You may perhaps walk for a whole day and see not a beast or a bird of any description. Yet they are here. Even in the lava-beds where not even cactus will grow, and where to all appearance there is no life whatever, you may see tracks in the sand where quail and road-runners and linnets have been running about in search of food. There

Tracks in the sand.

are tracks, too, of the coyote and the wild-cat—tracks following tracks. The animals and the birds belong to the desert or the neighboring mountains; but they are not always on view. You meet with them only in the early morning and evening when they are moving about. In the middle of the day they are in the shadow of bush or rock or lying in some cut bank or cave —keeping out of the direct rays of the sun. The birds are not very numerous even when *Scarcity of birds.* they come forth. They prefer places that afford better cover. And yet as you make a memorandum of each new bird you see you are surprised after a time to find how many are the varieties.

And the surprise grows when you think of the dangers and hardships that continually harass bird-life here in the desert. It may be *Dangers of bird-life.* fancied perhaps that the bird is exempt from danger because he has wings to carry him out of the reach of the animals; but we forget that he has enemies of his own kind in the air. And if he avoids the hawks by day, how shall he avoid the owls by night? Where at night shall *No cover for protection.* he go for protection? There are no broad-leaved trees to offer a refuge—in fact few trees of any sort. The bushes are not so high that a coyote cannot reach to their top at a jump ; nor are the spines and ledges of rock in the mountains so steep that a wild-cat cannot climb up them.

No ; the bird is subject to the same dangers as the animals and the plants. Something is forever on his trail. He must always be on guard. And the food problem, ever of vital interest to bird-life, bothers him just as much as it does the coyote. There is little for him to eat and nothing for him to drink ; and hardly a resting-place for the sole of his foot. Besides, it would seem as though he should be affected by the intense heat more than he is in reality. Humanity at times has difficulty in withstanding this heat, for though it is not suffocating, it parches the mouth and dries up the blood so rapidly that if water is not attainable the effect is soon apparent. The animals —that is, the wild ones—are never fazed by it ; but the domestic horse, dog, and cow yield to it almost as readily as a man. And men and animals are all of low-blood temperature—a man's normal temperature being about 98 F. But what of the bird in his coat of feathers which may add to or detract from his warmth ? What is his normal temperature ? It varies

The food problem.

The heat and drouth again.

with the species, so far as I can ascertain by experiment, from 112 to 120 F. Consider that blood temperature in connection with a surrounding air varying from 100 to 125 F. ! It would seem impossible for any life to support it. One may well wonder what strange wings beat this glowing air, what bird-life lives in this fiery waste !

A bird's temperature.

Yet the desert-birds look not very different from their cousins of the woods and streams except that they are thinner, more subdued in color, somewhat more alert. They are very pretty, very innocent-looking birds. But we may be sure that living here in the desert, enduring its hardships and participating in its incessant struggle for life and for the species, they have just the same savage instincts as the plants and the animals. The sprightliness and the color may suggest harmlessness ; but the eye, the beak, the claw are designed for destruction. The road-runner is one of the mildest-looking and most graceful birds of the desert, but the spring of the wild-cat to crush down a rabbit is not more fierce than the snap of the bird's beak as he tosses a luckless lizard. He is the only thing on the desert that has the temerity to fight a rattlesnake. It is said that he kills the

Innocent-looking birds with savage instincts.

The road-runner.

snake, but as to that I am not able to give evidence.

And it is not alone the bird of prey—not alone the road-runners, the eagles, the vultures, the hawks, and the owls that are savage of mood. Every little wisp of energy that carries a bunch of feathers is endowed with the same spirit. The downward swoop of the cactus wren upon a butterfly and the snip of his little scissors bill, the dash after insects of the fly-catchers, vireos, swallows, bats, and whippoor-wills are just as murderous in kind as the blow of the condor and the vice-like clutch of his talons as they sink into the back of a rabbit. Skill and strength in the chase are absolutely necessary in a desert where food is so scarce, and in proportion the little birds have these qualities in common with the great.

Wrens and fly-catchers.

And naturally, as in the case of the animals, the skill and the strength develop along the line of the bird's needs, producing that quality of character, that fitness for the work cut out for him, to which we have so often referred. There are birds that belong almost solely to the kingdom of the air—birds like the condor, the vulture, and the eagle. Upon the ground they move awkwardly, not having better feet to

Development of special characteristics.

walk with than ducks and geese. The talons
are too much developed for walking. When
they rise from the ground they do it heavily
and with quick flapping wings. Not until
they are fairly started in the upper air do
they show what wonderful wing-power they
possess.

Birds of the air.

The common brown-black vulture or turkey
buzzard is the type of all the wheelers and sail-
ers. The "soaring eagle" of poetry is something of a goose beside him. For the wings of
the vulture bear him through wind, sun, and
heat, hour after hour, without a pause. To
see him circling as he hunts down a mountain
range a hundred miles or more, one might
think that the abnormal breast-muscles never
grew weary. He goes over every foot of the
ground with his eyes and at the same time
watches every other vulture in the sky. Let
one of his fellows stop circling and drop earthward on a long incline, and immediately he is
followed by all the black crew. They know
instantly that something has been discovered.
But often the hunt is in vain, and then for
whole days at a time those motionless wings
bear their burden apparently without fatigue.
With no food perhaps for a fortnight and

The brown-black vulture.

The vulture hunting.

never any water, that spare rack of muscles sails the air with as little effort as floating thistle-down. No one knows just how it is done. In blow or calm, against the wind or with it, high in the blue or low over the ground, any place, anywhere, and under any circumstances those wings cut through the air almost like sunlight. You can hear a whizz like the flight of arrows as the bird passes close over your head; but you cannot see the slightest motion in the feathers.

The vulture sailing.

The hot, thin air of the desert would seem a less favorable air for sailing than the moister atmosphere of the south; but the vulture of the tropics is not the equal of the desert-bird. He is heavier, lazier, and more stupid—possibly because better fed. There are several varieties in the family, the chief variants being the one with white tipped wings and the one with a white eagle-like head. Neither of them is as good on the wing as the black species, though none of them is to be despised. Even the ordinary carrion crow of the desert is an expert sailer compared with any of the crow family to be found elsewhere. The exigencies of the situation seem to require wings developed for long-distance flights; and the vultures, the crows,

The southern buzzard.

The crow.

the eagles, the hawks, all respond after their
individual fashions.

The condor is perhaps the vulture's peer *The great condor.*
in the matter of sailing. He belongs to the
vulture family, though very much larger than
any of its members, sometimes measuring
fifteen feet across the wings and weighing forty
pounds. He is the largest bird on the continent. At the present time he is occasionally
seen wheeling high in air like a mere insect in
the great blue dome. It is said that he soars
as high as twentyfive thousand feet above the
earth. But to-day he sails alone and his tribe
has grown less year by year. With the eagles
he keeps well up in the high sierras and builds
a nest on the inaccessible peaks or along the
steep escarpments. He belongs to the desert
only because it is one of his hunting-grounds.

This may be said of the eagles and the hawks. *The eagles and hawks.*
They hunt the desert by day, but go home to
the mountains at night. The owls are somewhat different, not being given to long flight.
The deep caves or wind-worn recesses under
mountain ledges furnish them abiding-places.
These caves also send forth at dusk a full complement of bats that seem not different from
the ordinary Eastern bats. The burrowing

Bats and
owls.

owl is perhaps misnamed, though not misplaced.
There is no evidence whatever, that I have ever
seen or heard, to show that he burrows.   What
happens is that he crawls into some hole that is
already burrowed instead of a cave or recess in
the rocks.   A prairie-dog or badger hole is his
preference.   That the place has inhabitants,
including the tarantula and (it is said) the rattlesnake, does not bother the owl.   He walks
in with his mate and speedily makes himself at
home.   How the different families get on together can be imagined by one person as well as

The burrow-
ing owl.

by another.   They do not seem to pay any attention to each other so far as I have observed.
Ordinarily the desert animals, birds, and reptiles agree to no such truce.   They are at war
from the start.   I do not know that the owls,
the bats, the night-hawks have any special
equipment for carrying on their part of the
war.   Sometimes I have fancied they had larger
eyes than is usual with their kinds outside of
the desert ; but I have no proof of this.   Perhaps it is like the speculation as to whether the
buzzard sees or scents the carrion that he dis-
covers so readily—hardly amenable to proof.

All of the air-birds are strikingly developed
in the wings and equally undeveloped in the

feet, while all the ground-birds of the desert are just the reverse of this—that is, deficient in wings but strong of foot and leg. The road-runner, or as he is sometimes called the chap-arralcock, is a notable instance of this. He is a lizard-eater, and in order to eat he must first catch his lizard. Now this is by no means an easy task. The ordinary gray, brown, or yellow lizard is the swiftest dodger and darter there is in the sand, and even in straight-line running he will travel too fast for an ordinary dog to catch him. His facility, too, in dashing up, over, and under bowlders is not to be under-estimated. The road-runner's task then is not an easy one, and yet he seems to accomplish it easily. There is no great effort about his pursuit and yet he generally manages to catch the lizard. It is because his legs are specially constructed for running, and his head, neck, and beak for darting. His wings are of little use. When chased by a dog he will finally take to them, but only for about fifty yards. Then he drops to the ground and starts on foot again. He will run away from a man, and sometimes even a horse cannot keep up with him. Oddly enough, he seems always to run a little sideways. The long tail (used as a rudder) is car-

The ground birds.

The road-runner's swiftness.

ried a little to the right or the left and gives this impression. When frightened, his top-knot is raised like that of the pheasant, and he often runs with his beak open. It is a most vicious beak for all that it looks not more blood-thirsty than that of the crow. It snaps through a scorpion or a centipede like a pair of sheep-shearers. And with all his energy and strength the road-runner weighs only about a pound. He is a long-geared bird, but not actually any larger than a pigeon.

The blue valley-quail—whether of Arizona or California breeding—is quite as strong of leg as the road-runner, though not perhaps so swift. He does not care much about using his wings ; and at best they are not better than the rather poor average of quails' wings. By that I mean that all quails rise from cover with a great roar and bustle, and they fly very fast for a short distance ; but they are soon down upon the ground, running and hiding. The flight of the quail, too, is straight ahead. It is not possible for him to rise up over five hundred feet of canyon wall, for instance, and even on an ordinary mountain side he takes several flights before he reaches the summit. The wings are not muscled like the legs, and that is because

The vicious beak.

The desert-quail.

Wings of the quail.

the quail is a ground-bird. He gets his food there and spends most of his time there. In the East Bob White always roosts upon the ground, but the desert-quail is usually too clever to trust himself in such an exposed place. He will travel miles to get into a cotton-wood tree at dusk, and if there is water near at hand so much the better. He dearly loves the water and the tree, but if he cannot get them he accepts the situation philosophically and goes to sleep on a high ledge of rock with water perhaps in his thought but not in his crop.

Travelling for water.

Thanks to his capacity for travelling, the quail usually manages to get enough of small seeds and insects to keep himself alive. He is a great roamer—in the course of a day travelling over many miles of country—and his quest is always food. He likes to be among the great bowlders that lie along the bases of the mountains ; and when disturbed he flies and jumps from rock to rock, much to the discouragement of the coyote that happens to be the disturber. When forced to rise he flies perhaps for a hundred yards or more and then drops and begins running. In the spring he mates, raises a brood, and teaches the young ones the gentle art of running. In the fall he and his family

Habits of quail.

of a dozen or sixteen join with other families to make a great covey of several hundred, or in the old days before the market-hunters came, several thousand. And they all run. The bottom of the quail's foot is always itching for the ground ; and he seems never so happy as when leaving the enemy far behind him. His *His strong legs.* little legs take him through the brush so fast that you cannot keep up with him. Every muscle in him is as tough as a watch-spring. You may wound him, but you have not yet got him. He will creep into some cactus patch or crawl down a snake-hole—elude you in some way—and in the end die game just out of your reach.

There are few trees upon the desert and few bushes of any size ; yet there are birds of the *Bush-birds.* tree and the bush here just as there are birds of the air and the ground. The most of them seem the same kind of linnets, sparrows, and thrushes that are seen along the California coast ; though probably they have some peculiar desert characteristic. I cannot see any difference between the little woodpeckers here and the woodpeckers elsewhere ; yet this desert variety flies from sahuaro to sahuaro, alights on the spiny trunk with a little thump, and im-

mediately begins hitching himself up through
the worst imaginable rows of needles just as
though he were climbing a plain pine-tree.
The ordinary turtle-dove with his red pigeon-
feet alights on the top of the same sahuaro,
the wren bores holes in it and makes a nest
within the cylinder ; and the dwarf thrush
dashes in and out of tangled thickets of cholla
all day long, and yet none of them suffers any
injury. It seems incredible that birds not accustomed to the desert could do such things.

The wood-peckers and cactus.

Possibly, too, these bush-birds — insect-de-
vourers most of them—have some special faculty
for catching their prey, though I have not been
able to discover it. The fly-catchers, the mocking-birds, the finches, in a land of plenty are
quick enough in breaking the back of a butterfly or beetle, and any extra energy would seem
superfluous. Still there is no telling what fine
extra stimulus lies in an empty crop. And
crops are usually empty on the desert. Even
the little humming-bird has difficulty in pick-
ing a living. In blossom time he is, of course,
in fine condition, but I have seen him dashing
about in the fall when nothing at all was in
bloom, and evidently none the worse for some
starvation. He is a swifter flyer than the or-

Finches and mocking-birds.

The hum-ming-bird.

dinary bird and is also duller in coloring, but in other respects he seems not different. He breeds on the desert, building his nest in the pitahaya ; and he and his mate then have a standing quarrel with their neighbors for the rest of the summer. There is not in the whole feathered tribe a more quarrelsome scrap of vivacity than the humming-bird.

Doves and grosbeaks.

The dwarf dove common to Sonora, the oven-bird, the red grosbeak, and many other of the smaller birds known to civilization, are found on the desert ; but apparently with no special faculty for overcoming its hardships. This is due perhaps to the fact that they are not always there — are not exclusively desert-birds. Nor do any of the migratory birds belong to the desert, though they stop here for weeks at a time in their flights north or south. At almost any season of the year one sees the cow-blackbird and the smaller crow-blackbird. The mocking-bird comes only in the spring and fall, and the lark in early summer. The lark looks precisely like the Eastern bird, but his note is changed ; whereas the flicker has changed the color under his wings from yellow to pink, but not his note. The robin is no whit different from the front-lawn robin of

The lark and flicker.

our childhood; and the bobolink rising from
salt-bush and yucca, singing as he rises, is the
bobolink of ancient days. At times there are
troops of magpies that come and go across the *Jays and*
waste, and at other times troops of blue-jays. *magpies.*
And high in air through the warmth of spring
and the cold of autumn there are great flocks
of ducks, geese, brant, divers, shags, willet, *Water-fowl.*
curlew, swinging along silently to the southern
or northern waterways. They seldom pause,
even when following the Colorado River, unless
in need of water. On the mesas and uplands
one sometimes sees a group of sand-hill cranes
walking about and indulging in a crazy dance
peculiarly their own, but the sight is no longer a common one.

And again the prey—what of the prey? Has
Nature left the beetles, the bugs, the worms, *Beetles and*
the bees, completely at the pleasure of the bird's *worms.*
beak? No; not completely, though it must
be acknowledged that she has not provided
much defensive armor for them individually.
She incases her beautiful blue and yellow
beetles in hard shells that other insects cannot
break through, but they are flimsy defences
against the mocking-bird. To bugs and worms
and bees she gives perhaps a sting, deadly

enough when thrust into a spider, but useless again when used in defence against a cactus-thrush. And this is where Nature shows her absolute indifference to the life or the death of the individual. She allows the bugs and beetles to be slaughtered like the mackerel in the sea. But she is a little more careful about preserving the species. And how does she do this without preserving the individual ? Why, simply by increasing the number of individuals, by breed, by fertility, by multiplicity. Thousands are annually slaughtered ; yes, but thousands are annually bred. What matter about their lives or deaths provided they do not increase or decrease as a species !

Fighting destruction by breed.

The insects on the desert are mere flashes of life—pin-points of energy—but not without purpose and not without beauty. The beasts and the birds may be bleached brown or gray by the sun ; but the insects are many of them as gay as those of the tropics. The ordinary beetles that a chance turn of a stone reveals are like scarabs of gold, turquoise, azurite, bronze, platinum, hurrying and scurrying out of the way. The tarantula-wasp, with his gorgeous orange-colored body and his blue wings, is like a bauble made of precious stones flickering along

The blue and green beetles.

the ground. The great dragon-fly with his
many lensed eyes, the bees with black and yellow bodies, the butterflies with bright-hued *Butterflies.*
wings, the white and gray millers—all of them
dwellers in the sands—are spots of light and
color that illumine the desert as the rich jewel
the Ethiop's ear. The wings of gauze that
bear the ordinary fly upon the air, the feet of
ebony that carry the plain black beetle along the
rocks, are made with just as much care and skill
as the wings of the condor and the foot of the
road-runner. Nature in every product of her
hand shows the completeness of her workman-
ship. She made the wings and the legs for a
purpose and they fulfil that purpose. They
are without flaw and above reproach. Once *Design and*
character.
more, therefore, have they character and fitness,
and once more, therefore, are they beautiful.

I need not now argue beauty in the birds, *Beauty of*
birds.
the beetles, and the butterflies. You will admit
it without argument. The slate-blue of the
quail, the gay red of the grosbeak, the charm
of the rock-wren, the vivacity of the bobolink or
the scale-runner, captivate you and compel your
sympathy and admiration. Yes ; but everyone
of them is, after his kind, as much of a butcher,
just as much of a destroyer, as the wild-cat or

the yellow rattlesnake. And they have no more
character and perhaps less fitness for the desert
life than the sneaking coyote or the flattened
lizard which you do not admire. But why are
not the coyote and the lizard beautiful too ?

Beauty also of reptiles. Why not the beauty of the horned toad and the
serpent ? Are we never to love or to admire
save where form and color tickle the eye ? Are
these forever to monopolize the name of beauty
and gather to themselves the world's applause ?

If we could but rid ourselves of the false ideas,
which, taken *en masse*, are called education, we
should know that there is nothing ugly under
the sun, save that which comes from human

Nature's work all purposeful. distortion. Nature's work is all of it good, all
of it purposeful, all of it wonderful, all of it
beautiful. We like or dislike certain things
which may be a way of expressing our prejudice
or our limitation ; but the work is always perfect of its kind irrespective of human appreci-
ation. We may prefer the sunlight to the starlight, the evening primrose to the bisnaga, the
antelope to the mountain-lion, the mocking-bird
to the lizard ; but to say that one is good and
the other bad, that one is beautiful and the other
ugly, is to accuse Nature herself of preference—
something which she never knew. She designs

for the cactus of the desert as skilfully and as
faithfully as for the lily of the garden.   Each
in its way is suited to its place, and each in its
way has its unique beauty of character.   And
so, more truly perhaps than Shakespeare himself knew, the toad called ugly and venomous,
still holds a precious jewel in its head.

*Precious
jewel of the
toad.*

CHAPTER XI

MESAS AND FOOT-HILLS

THE word mesa (table), by local usage in Mexico and in the western United States, is applied to any flat tract of ground that lies above an arroyo or valley, as well as to the flat top of a mountain. In a broad, if somewhat strained use of the word, it also means the great table-lands and elevated plains lying between a river-valley and the mountain confines on either side of it. The mesas are the steps or benches that lead upward from the river to the mountain, though the resemblance to benches is not always apparent because of the cuttings and washings of intermittent streams, and the breakings and crossings of mountain-spurs.

Flat steps of the desert.

As you rise up from the Colorado Desert, crossing the river to the east, you meet with a great plain or so-called mesa that extends far across Southern Arizona and Sonora almost up to the Continental Divide. It is broken by

Across Southern Arizona.

194

short ranges of barren mountains, that have the general trend of the main Sierra Madre, and it looks so much like the country to the west of the river that it is usually recognized as a part of the desert, or at the least "desert country."

It is, however, somewhat different from the Bottom of the Bowl or even the valleys of the Mojave. The elevation, for one thing, gives it another character. The rise from bench to bench is very gradual, and to the ordinary observer hardly perceptible; but nevertheless when the foot-hills of the Santa Rita Mountains are reached, the altitude is four thousand feet or more. There is a difference in light, sky, color, air; even some change in the surface of the earth. The fine sands of the lower desert and the sea-bed silts are missing; the mesas lie close up to the mountains and receive the first coarse wash from the sides; the barrancas on the mountain - sides are choked with great masses of fallen rock, with bowlders of granite, with blocks of blackened lava. The arroyos that carry the wash from the mountains—mere ditches and trenches cut through the mesas— are filled with rounded stones, coarse sands, glittering scales of mica, bits of quartz, breaks

Rising up from the desert.

The great mesas.

of agate and carnelian. The mesas themselves
are made up of sand and gravel, sometimes
long shelvings of horizontal rocks, sometimes
patches of terra-cotta, rifts of copper shale,
or beds of parti-colored clay.

There is more rain in this upland country
and consequently more vegetation than down
below. Grease wood grows everywhere and is
the principal green thing in sight. So pre-
dominant is it that the term "grease wood
plains" is not inappropriate to the whole region. Groves of sahuaro stand in the valleys
and reach up and over the mountain-tops,
chollas and nopals are on the flats; the mesquite grows in miniature forests. But besides
these there are bushes and trees not seen in the
basin. Palo fierro, palo blanco, cottonwood
live along the dry river-beds, white and black
sage on the mesas, white and black oaks in the
foot-hills. Then, too, there are patches of pale
yellow sun-dried grass covering many acres,
great beds of evening primrose, and fields covered with the purple salt-bush. It is quite another country when you come to examine it
piece by piece.

As you rise higher and higher to the Continental Divide the whole face of the mesa under-

"Grease wood" plains.

Upland vegetation.

goes a further change. It slips imperceptibly
into a grass plain, stretching flat as far as the *Grass
plains.*
eye can see, covered with whitened grass, and
marked by clumps of yuccas slowly growing
into yucca palms. No rocks, trees, cacti, or
grease wood ; no primrose, wild gourd, or verbena. Nothing but yucca palms, bleached
grass, blue sky, and lilac mountains. It is still
in kind a desert country, and it is still called a
mesa or table-land ; but its character is changed
into something like the great flat lands of Ne-
braska or the broken plateau country of Montana.

In the spring, when the snows have melted *Spring and
summer on
the plains.*
and the rains have fallen, these plains turn
green with young grass and are spattered with
great patches of wild-flowers ; but the drouth
and heat of early summer soon fade the grasses
to a bright yellow, and in the fall the yellow
bleaches to a dead white. There is little wild
life left upon these plains. The bush-birds
need more cover than is to be found here, while
the ground-birds need more open roadway.
In the spring, when the prairie pools are filled
with water, there are geese and cranes in abundance ; but they soon pass on north. These
great grass tracts were once the home of count-

less bands of antelope, for it is just such an open country as the antelope loves; but they have passed on, too. In their place roam herds of cattle, and the gray wolf, the coyote, and the buzzard follow the herds.

The grease wood and the grass plains of Arizona and New Mexico are typical of all the flat countries lying up from the deserts; and yet there are many tracts of small acreage in this same region that show distinctly different features. Sometimes there are small beds of flat alkali dust, sometimes beds of soda and gypsum, sometimes beds of salt. Then occasionally there is a broad plain sown broadcast far and wide with blocks of lava—the remnants of a great lava-stream sent forth many centuries ago; and again flat reaches strewn thick with blocks of porphyry that have been washed down from the mountains no one knows just when or how. You are always riding into the unexpected in these barren countries, stumbling upon strange phenomena, seeing strange sights.

And yet as you ascend from the valley of the Colorado moving to the northeast, the lands and the sights become even stranger. For now you are rising to the Great Plateau and the Grand Canyon country—the region of the butte, the vast escarpment, the dome, the cliff, the gorge. It is a more mountainous land than that lying to the south, and it is deeper cut with river-beds and canyons. Yet still you have no trouble in finding even here the flat spaces peculiar to all the desert-bordering territory. There are grease wood plains as at the south and great bare benches that seem endless in their sweep. There are, too, spaces covered with lava-blocks and beds of soda and salt. More rain falls here than at the south or west; and in certain sections the grass grows rank, the yuccas become trees, and higher up toward Ash Fork the hills are covered with a growth of juniper. Flowers and shrubs are more abundant, birds and animals come and go across your pathway, and there are green valleys with water running upon the surface of the ground. And yet not twenty miles from the green valley you may enter upon the most barren plain imaginable—a place like the Painted Desert, perhaps, where in spots not a living thing of any kind is seen, where there is nothing but dry rock in the mountains and dry dust in the valley. These areas of utter desolation are of frequent enough occurrence in all the regions lying immediately to the north and the east of the Mojave to re-

The Grand Canyon country.

Hills covered with juniper.

The Painted Desert.

mind you that you are still in a desert land, and that the bench and the arid plain are really a part of the great waste itself.

Riding on the mesas.

Nature never designed more fascinating country to ride over than these plains and mesas lying up and back from the desert basin. You may be alone without necessarily being lonesome. And everyone rides here with the feeling that he is the first one that ever broke into this unknown land, that he is the original discoverer; and that this new world belongs to him by right of original exploration and conquest. Life becomes simplified from necessity.

The reversion to savagery.

It begins all over again, starting at the primitive stage. There is a reversion to the savage. Civilization, the race, history, philosophy, art—how very far away and how very useless, even contemptible, they seem. What have they to do with the air and the sunlight and the vastness of the plateau ! Nature and her gift of buoyant life are overpowering. The joy of mere animal existence, the feeling that it is good to be alive and face to face with Nature's self, drives everything else into the background.

The thin air again.

And what air one breathes on these plains—what wonderful air ! It is exhilarating to the whole body ; it brightens the senses and sweetens the mind and quiets the nerves. And how clear it is ! Leagues away needle and spine and mountain-ridge still come out clear cut against the sky. Is it the air alone that makes possible such far-away visions, or has the light somewhat to do with it ? What penetrating, all-pervading, wide-spread light ! How silently it falls and how like a great mirror the plain reflects it back to heaven !

Light and air—what means wherewith to conjure up illusions and deceive the senses ! We think we see far away a range of low hills, but, as we ride on, buttes and lomas seem to detach and come toward us. There is no range ahead of us ; there are only scattered groups of hills many miles apart. Far away to the left on a little rise of ground is a wild horse watching us, his head high in air, his nostrils sniffing for our scent upon the breeze. How colossal he seems ! Doubtless he is the last of some upland band, the leader of the troop who through great size and strength was best fitted to survive. But no ; he is only a common little Indian pony distorted to huge proportions by the heated atmosphere. We are riding into the sunset. Ahead of us every notch in the hills, every little valley has a shaft of golden light streaming

The light and its deceptions.

Distorted proportions.

through it. But turn in your saddle and look to the east, and the hills we have left behind us are surrounded by veilings of lilac. Again the omnipresent desert air! We see the western hills as through an amber glass, but looking to the east the glass is changed to pale amethyst.

Changed colors.

How delicately beautiful are the hills that seem to gather in little groups along the waste! They are not sharp-edged in their ridges like the higher mountains. Wind, rain, and sand have done their work upon them until there is hardly a rough feature left to them. All their lines are smooth and flow from one into another; and all the parti-colors of their rocks and soils are blended into one tone by the light and the air. With surfaces that catch and reflect light, and little depressions that hold shadows, how very picturesque they are! Indeed as you watch them breaking the horizon-line you are surprised to see how easily they compose into pictures. If you tried to put them upon canvas your surprise would probably be greater to find how very little you could make of them. The desert is not more paintable than the Alps. Both are too big.

The little hills.

Painting the desert.

These hills—they are usually called lomas—

that one meets with in the plateau region are not of the same make-up as the clay buttes of Wyoming or the gravel hills of New England. They have a core of rock within them and are nothing less than washed-down foot-hills. You will often see a chain of them receding from the range toward the plain, and growing smaller as they recede, until the last one is a mound only a few feet in height. They are flattening down to the level of the plain—sinking into the sandy sea.

Worn-down mountains.

Usually the lomas are seen against a background of dark mountains of which they are or have been at one time a constituent part. For the lomas are the outliers from the foot-hills as the foot-hills from the mountains proper. They are the most worn because they are the lowest down in the valley—in fact the bottom steps which receive not only their own wash but that of all the other steps besides. The mountains pour their waters and loose stones upon the foot-hills, the foot-hills cast them off upon the lomas, and the lomas in turn thrust them upon the plains. But the casting off effort becomes weaker at each step as the sides of the hill become less of a declivity. When the little hill is reached the sand-wash settles about the

The mountain-wash and its effect.

Flattening down to the plain.

base, and in time the whole mass rises on its sides and sinks somewhat in the centre, until a mere rise of ground is all that remains. So perish the hills that we are accustomed to speak of as "everlasting." It is merely another illustration of Nature's method in the universe. She is as careless of the individual hill or mountain as of the individual man, animal, or flower. All are beaten into dust. But the species is more enduring, better preserved. Year by year Nature is tearing down, washing down, pulling to pieces range after range ; but year by year

Mountain-making.

she is also heaving up stupendous mountains like the Alps, and crackling with a mighty squeeze the earth's crust into the ridges of the Rockies and the Andes.

The foot-hills.

The foot-hills are just what their name indicates—the hills that lie at the foot of the mountains. They are not usually detached from the main range like so many of the lomas, but are a part of it ; and while not exactly the buttresses of the mountains, yet they remind one of those architectural supports of cathedral walls. The foot-hills themselves are perhaps as firmly supported as the mountains for very often they stretch down from the mountains in a long ridge like a spine, and from the spine are

thrown out supporting ribs that trail away into
the valleys. In a granite country these foot-
hills are usually very smooth, and are made up
largely, as regards their surfaces, of the grit and
grind of the rocks. The rocks themselves are
usually wind worn, rounded by rain and sand,
and sometimes fantastic in shape. Often the
soft granite wears through in seams and leaves
lozenge-like blocks linked together like beads
upon a string ; often the whole rock-crown of
the hill is honey-combed by the wind until it
looks as soft as a sponge. The foot-hills of
porphyry are more jagged and rough in every
way. The stone is much harder and while it
splits like granite and falls along the mountain-
side in a talus it does not readily disintegrate.
The last bit of it remains a hard kernel, and
the porphyry foot-hill is usually a keen-edged
mountain in miniature.

Forms of the foot-hills.

The hills have a desert vegetation of grease
wood, cactus, and sage, with occasional trees like
the palo verde and the lluvia d'oro ; but their
general appearance is not very different from
the mesas. Where the altitude is high—say
five thousand feet and over—there may be a
more radical change in vegetation ; for now the
oak begins to appear, and if it is open country

Mountain-plants.

the grasses and flowers show everywhere. Sometimes the foot-hills are covered with a dense
chaparral made up of many low trees and
bushes; but this growth is more peculiar to
the Californian hills west of the Coast Range
than to Arizona. Many of the ranges in the

Bare
mountains.
Canyon country are almost as bare of vegetation as an ancient lake-bed. And sometimes
altitude seems to have little to do with the
kinds of growths. Cacti and the salt-bush
flourish at six thousand feet as readily as down
in the Salton Basin three hundred feet below
sea-level. The most dangerous and difficult
thing to set up about anything in this desert
world is the general law or common rule. The
exception—the thing that is perhaps uncom-
mon—comes up at every turn to your undoing.

Even the mountains of Arizona that have an
elevation of from five to eight thousand feet
are often quite bare of timber. The sahuaro,
the nopal, the palo verde may grow to their
very peaks and still make only a scanty cover-

The
southern
exposures.
ing. Seen from a distance the southern exposure of the mountain looks perfectly bare;
but if you travel around it to the north side
where the sunlight does not fall except for a

few hours of the day, you will find a growth of bushes, small trees, vines, and grasses that, taken together, form something of a thicket—that is for a desert. And here, too, on the northern exposure you will find the abrupt walls of the peak stained with great fields of orange and gray lichens that lend a color quality to the whole top.

Gray lichens.

But through the bushes and grasses and lichens the wine-red of the porphyry comes cropping out to tell you that the mountain is a mass of rock, that it holds little or no soil on its sides, that it has not a suspicion of water; and that whatever grows upon it, does so, not by favor of circumstance, but through sheer desert stubbornness. The vegetation is a thin disguise that is penetrated in a few moments. The arid character of the mountain says plainly enough that we are not yet out of the region of sands and burning winds and fiery sun-shafts. The whole of the Arizona country as far east as the Continental Divide, in spite of its occasional green valleys and few high mountain-ranges with timbered tops, is a slope leading up and out from the desert by gradual if broken steps which we have called mesas or benches. It is a bare, dry land. Its name would imply

Still in the desert region.

that the early Spaniards had found it that and

Arida zona. called it *arida zona* for cause.*

Yet at times it is a land of heavy cloud-bursts and wash-outs. In the summer months it frequently rains on the mesas in torrents. The bare surface of the country drains this water almost like the roof of a house because there are

Cloud-bursts on the mesas. no grasses or bushes of consequence to check the water and allow it to soak into the ground. The descent from the Divide to the Colorado River is quite steep. The flood of waters rushes down the steps of the mesas and over the bare ground with terrific force. It quickly cuts channels in the low places down which are hurled sand, gravel, and bowlders. The cutting

The wash of rains. of the channel during the heavy rains is something extraordinary, partly because the stream has great volume and fall, and partly because the channel-bed is usually of soft rock and easily cut. In a few dozen years the arroyo of a mesa that carries off the water from the mountain-range has cut a river-bed many feet deep ; in a

* The late Dr. Elliot Coues and others reject the obvious *arida zona* of the Spanish in favor of some strained etymologies from the Indian dialects, about which no two of them agree. Why should the name not have come from the Spanish, and why should it not mean just simply arid zone or belt ?

few hundred years the valley-bed changes into a gorge with five hundred feet of sheer rock-wall ; in a few thousand years perhaps the restless wearing water of the great river has sunk its bed five thousand feet below the surface and made the Grand Canyon of the Colorado. *Gorge cutting.*

The Canyon country is well named, for it has plenty of wash-outs and gorges. Almost anywhere among the mountain-ranges you can find them—not Grand Canyons, to be sure, but ones of size sufficient to be impressive without being stupendous. Walls of upright rock several hundred feet in height have enough bulk and body about them to impress anyone. The mass is really overpowering. It is but the crust of the earth exposed to view ; but the gorge at Niagara and the looming shaft of the Matterhorn are not more. The imagination strains at such magnitude. And all the accessories of the gorge and canyon have a might to them that adds to the general effect. The sheer precipices, the leaning towers, the pinnacles and shafts, the recesses and caves, the huge basins rounded out of rock by the waterfalls are all touched by the majesty of the sublime. *In the canyons.* *Upright walls of rock.*

And what could be more beautiful than the deep shadow of the canyon ! You may have

*Color in
canyon
shadows.*

had doubts about those colored shadows which
painters of the *plein-air* school talked so much
about a few years ago.   You may have thought
that it was all talk and no reality ; but now that
you are in the canyon, and in a shadow, look
about you and see if there is not plenty of color
there, too.   The walls are dyed with it, the
stones are stained with it—all sorts of colors
from strata of rock, from clays and slates, from
minerals, from lichens, from mosses.   The
stones under your feet have not turned black
or brown because out of the sunlight.   If you
were on the upper rim of the canyon looking
down, the whole body of air in shadow would
look blue.   And that strange light coming from
above !   You may have had doubts, too, about

*The blue sky
seen from
the canyon
depths.*

the intense luminosity of the blue sky ; but look
up at it along the walls of rock to where it
spreads in a thin strip above the jaws of the
canyon.   Did you ever see such light coming
out of the blue before !   See how it flashes from
the long line of tumbling water that pitches over
the rocks !   White as an avalanche, the water
slips through the air down to its basin of stone ;
and white, again, as the snow are the foam and
froth of the pool.

Stones and water in a gorge, wastes of rock

thrust upward into mountains, long vistas of plain and mesa glaring in the sunlight—what things are these for a human being to fall in love with ? Doctor Johnson, who occasionally went into the country to see his friends, but never to see the country, who thought a man demented who enjoyed living out of town ; and who cared for a tree only as firewood or lumber, what would he have had to say about the desert and its confines ? In his classic time, *Desert landscape.* and in all the long time before him, the earth and the beauty thereof remained comparatively unnoticed and unknown. Scott, Byron, Hugo, —not one of the old romanticists ever knew Nature except as in some strained way symbolic *The former knowledge of Nature.* of human happiness or misery. Even when the naturalists of the last half of the nineteenth century took up the study they were impressed at first only with the large and more apparent beauties of the world—the Alps, the Niagaras, the Grand Canyons, the panoramic views from mountain-tops. They never would have tolerated the desert for a moment.

But the Nature-lover of the present, who has taken so kindly to the minor beauties of the world, has perhaps a little wider horizon than his predecessors. Not that his positive knowledge is so much greater, but rather where he lacks in knowledge he declines to condemn.

The Nature-lover of the present.

He knows now that Nature did not give all her energy to the large things and all her weakness to the small things; he knows now that she works by law and labors alike for all; he knows now that back of everything is a purpose, and if he can discover the purpose he cannot choose but admire the product.

That is something of an advance no doubt—a grasp at human limitations at least—but there is no reason to think that it will lead to any lofty heights. Nature never intended that we

Human limitations.

should fully understand. That we have stumbled upon some knowledge of her laws was more accident than design. We have by some strange chance groped our way to the Gate of the Garden, and there we stand, staring through the closed bars, with the wonder of little children. Alas! we shall always grope! And shall we ever cease to wonder?

CHAPTER XII

MOUNTAIN-BARRIERS

THE character of the land lying along the western boundaries of the deserts is very different from that of the Arizona canyon country. Moving toward the Pacific you meet with no mesas of consequence, nor do you traverse many plateaus or foot-hills. The sands extend up to the bases of the Coast Range and then stop short. The mountains rise abruptly from the desert like a barrier or wall. Sometimes they lift vertically for several thousand feet, but more often they present only a steep rough grade. There are cracks in the wall called passes, through which railways lead on to the Pacific ; and there are high divides and saddles —dips in the top of the wall—through which in the old days the Indians trailed from desert to sea, and which are to-day known only to the inquisitive few.

The western mountains.

Saddles and passes.

From the saddles—and better still from the topmost peaks—there are wonderful sights to

be seen. You will never know the vast reach
of the deserts until you see them from a point
of rock ten thousand feet in air. Then you are
standing on the Rim of the Bowl and can see
the yellow ocean of sand within and the blue
ocean of water without. The ascent to that
high point is, however, not easy, especially if
undertaken from the desert side. But nothing
could be more interesting in quick change and
new surprise than the rise from the hot waste
at the bottom to the cold white-capped peaks of
the top. It is not often that you find mountains with their feet thrust into tropic sands
and their heads thrust into clouds of snow.

*The view
from the
mountain-
top.*

Before you start to climb, before you reach
the foot of the mountains, you are struck by
the number of dry washes leading down from
the sides and gradually losing themselves in the
sands. As the eyes trace these arroyos up the
mountain-side they are seen to turn into green
streaks and finally, near the peak, into white
streaks. You know what that means and yet
can hardly believe that those white lines are
snow-banks packed many feet deep in the canyons ; that from them run streams which
lower down become green lines because of the
grasses, bushes, and trees growing on their

*Looking up
toward the
peak.*

banks; and that finally the streams, after plunging through canyons, fall into the arroyos and are drunk up by the desert sands before they have left the mountain-bases. It seems incredible that a stream should be born; run its course through valley, gorge, and canyon; and then disappear forever in the sands, all within a few miles. Yet not one but many of these mountain-streams have that brief history.

Lost streams.

And at one time they must have been larger, or there were slips of glaciers or avalanches on the mountains; for the arroyos are piled with great blocks of granite and there are rows of bowlders on either side which might have been rolled there by floods or pushed there by an ice-sheet. As you draw nearer, the bowlders crop out in large fields and beds. They surround the rock bases like a deposit rather than a talus, and over them one must pass on his way up the mountain-side.

Avalanches and bowl-der-beds.

If you ascend by the bed of the arroyo it is not long before you begin to note the presence of underground water. It is apparent in the green of the vegetation. The grasses are seen growing first in bunches and then in sods, little blue flowers are blooming beside the grasses; alders, willows, and young sycamores

The ascent by the arroyo.

are growing·along the banks, and live-oaks are
in the stream-bed among the bowlders. As you
move up and into the mountain the bed becomes more of a rocky floor, the earth-deposits
grow thinner, and presently little water-pockets
begin to show themselves. At first you see
them in pot-holes and worn basins in the rock,
Growth of the stream. then water begins to show in small pools under
cut banks, and then perhaps there is a little
glassy slip of light over a flat rock in a narrow
section of the bed. Gradually the slip grows in
length and joins the pools, until at last you
see the stream come to life, as it were, out of
the ground.

Rising banks. The banks begin to rise. As you advance
they lift higher and higher, they grow into
abrupt walls of rock ; the strata of granite crop
out in ragged ledges. The trees and grasses
disappear, and in their place come cold pale
flowers growing out of beds of moss, or cling-
ing in rock-niches where all around the gray
and orange lichens are weaving tapestries upon
the walls. The bed of the stream seems to have
sunken down, but in reality it is rising by steps
Waterfalls. and falls ever increasing in size. The stream
itself has grown much larger, swifter, more
noisy. You move slowly up and around the

falls, each one harder to surmount than the last, until finally you are in the canyon.

The walls are high, the air is damp, the light is dim. The glare and heat of the desert have vanished and in their place is the shadow of the cave. You toil on far up the chasm, creeping along ledges and rising by niches, until a great pool, a basin hewn from the rock, is before you ; and the hewer is seen waving and flashing in the air a hundred feet as it falls into the pool. Around you and ahead of you is a sheer pitch of rock curved like a horseshoe. It is insurmountable ; there is no thoroughfare. You will not gain the peak by way of the canyon. The water-ousel on the basin edge—sole tenant of the gorge—seems to laugh at your ignorance of that fact. Let us turn back and try the ridges. *In the gorge.*

Up the faces of the spurs and thus by the backbones and saddles to the summit is not easy travelling. At first desert vegetation surrounds you, for the cacti and all their companions creep up the mountain-side as far as possible. The desert does not give up its dominion easily. Bowlders are everywhere, vines and grasses are growing under their shade ; and, as you advance, the bushes arise and gradually *The ascent by the ridges.*

thicken into brush, and the brush runs into a chaparral. The manzanita, the lavender, and white lilac, the buckthorn, the laurel, the sumac, all throw out stiff dry arms that tear at your clothing. The mountain-covering that from below looked an ankle-deep of grasses and weeds—a velvety carpet only—turns out to be a dense tangle of brush a dozen feet high. It is not an attractive place because the only successful method of locomotion through it is on the hands and knees. That method of moving is peculiar to the bear, and so for that matter *The chaparral.* is the chaparral through which you are tearing your way. It is one of the hiding-places of the *Home of the grizzly.* grizzly. And there are plenty of grizzlies still left in the Sierra Madre. To avoid the chaparral (and also the bear) you would better keep on the sunny side of the spurs where the ground is more open.

You are at the top of one of the outlying spurs *Ridge trails and taluses.* at last and you find there a dim trail made by deer and wolves leading along the ridge, across the saddle, and up to the next spur. As you follow this you presently emerge from the brush and come face to face with a declivity, covered by broken blocks of stone that seem to have been slipping down the mountain-side for cen-

turies. It is an old talus of one of the spurs.
You wind about it diagonally until different
ground is reached, and then you are once more
upon a ridge—higher by a spur than before.

Again the scene changes. An open park-
like country appears covered with tall grass,
the sunlight flickers on the shiny leaves of live-
oaks, and dotted here and there are tall yuccas
in bloom—the last of the desert growths to
vanish from the scene. Flowers strange to the
desert are growing in the grass—clumps of yellow violets, little fields of pink alfileria, purple
lilies, purple nightshades, red paint-brushes,
and flaming fire-rods. And there are birds in the
trees that know the desert only as they fly—blue
birds with red breasts as in New England, blue-
jays with their chatter as in Minnesota, blue-
backed woodpeckers with their tapping on dead
limbs as in Pennsylvania. And here was once
the stamping-ground of the mule-deer. Here
in the old days under the shade of the live-oak
he would drowse away the heat of the day and
at night perhaps step down to the desert. He
was safe then in the open country, but to-day
he knows danger and skulks in the depths of
the chaparral, from which a hound can scarcely
drive him.

*Among the
live-oaks.*

*Birds and
deer.*

Onward and upward through the oaks until you are on the top of another ridge. Did you think it was the top because it hid the peak? Ah no; the granite crags are still far above you. And there, yawning at your very feet, is another canyon whose existence you never suspected. How steep and broad and ragged the walls look to you! And down in the bottom of the canyon—almost a mile down it seems—are huge masses of rock, fallen towers and ledges, great frost-heaved strata lying piled in confusion among trees and vines and heavy brush. Here and there down the canyon's length appear disconnected flashes of silvery light showing where a stream is dashing its way under rocks and through tangled brush down to the sandy sea. And far above you to the right where the canyon heads is a streak of dirty-looking snow. There is nothing for it but to get around the head of the canyon above the snow-streak, for crossing the canyon itself is unprofitable, not to say impossible.

How odd it seems after the sands to see the snow. The long wedge lying in the barranca under the shadowed lee of an enormous spur is not very inviting looking. It has melted down and accumulated dust and dirt until it looks al-

Yawning canyons.

The canyon stream.

Snow.

most like a bed of clay. But the little stream running away from its lowest part is pure ; and it dashes through the canyon, tumbles into little pools, and slips over shelving precipices like a thing of life. Could the canyon have been cut out of the solid rock by that little stream ? Who knows ! Besides, the stream is not always so small. The descent is steep, and bowlders carried down by great floods cut faster than water.

The wear of water.

It is dangerous travelling — this crossing of snow-banks in June. You never know how soft they may be nor how deep they may drop you. Better head the snow-bank no matter how much hard brush and harder stones there may be to fight against. The pines are above you and they are beginning to appear near you. Beside you is a solitary shaft of dead timber, its branches wrenched from it long ago and its trunk left standing against the winds. And on the ground about you there are fallen trunks, crumbled almost to dust, and near them young pines springing up to take the place of the fallen. Manzanita and buckthorn and lilac are here, too ; but the chaparral is not so dense as lower down. You pass through it easily and press on upward, still upward, in the cool mountain-air, until you are above the barranca of snow and un-

The pines.

Barrancas and escarpments.

der the lee of a vast escarpment. The wall is perpendicular and you have to circle it looking for an exit higher up. For half an hour you move across a talus of granite blocks, and then through a break in the wall you clamber up to the top of the escarpment. You are on a high spur which leads up a pine-clad slope. You are coming nearer your quest.

The pines!—at last the pines! How gigantic they seem, those trees standing so calm and majestic in their mantles of dark green—how gigantic to eyes grown used to the little palo verde or the scrubby grease wood! All classes

Under the pines.

of pines are here—sugar pines, bull pines, white pines, yellow pines—not in dense numbers standing close together as in the woods of Oregon, but scattered here and there with open aisles through which the sunshine falls in broad

Bushes, ferns, and mosses.

bars. Many small bushes—berry bushes most of them—are under the pines; and with them are grasses growing in tufts, flowers growing in beds, and bear-clover growing in fields. Aimless and apparently endless little streams wander everywhere, and ferns and mosses go with them. Bowlder streams they are, for the rounded bowlder is still in evidence—in the stream, on the bank, and under the roots of the pine.

The beautiful mountain-quail loves to scramble over these stones, especially when they are in the water; and the mountain-quail is here. This is his abiding-place, and you are sure to see him, for he has a curiosity akin to that of the antelope and must get on a bowlder or a log to look at you. And this is the home of hundreds of woodpeckers that seem to spend their entire lives in pounding holes in the pine-trees and then pounding acorns into the holes. It is a very thrifty practice and provides against winter consumption, only the squirrels consume the greater part of the acorns if the blue-jays do not get ahead of them. For here lives the ordinary blue-jay and also his mountain cousin, the crested jay, with a coat so blue that it might better be called indigo. A beautiful bird, but with a jangling note that rasps the air with discord. His chief occupation seems to be climbing pine-trees as by the rungs of a ladder. There are sweeter notes from the warblers, the nuthatches, and the chickadees. But no desert-bird comes up so high; and as for the common lawn and field birds like the robin and the thrush, they do not fancy the pines.

Upward, still upward, under the spreading arms of the pines! How silent the forest save

Mountain-quail.

Indigo jays.

Warblers.

for the soughing of the wind through the pine needles and the jangle of the jays! And how thin and clear the mountain-air! How white the sunlight falling upon the moss-covered rocks! It must be that we have risen out of the dust-laden atmosphere of the desert. And out of its heat too. The air feels as though blown to us from snow-banks, and indeed, they are in the gullies lying on either side of us. For now we are coming close to the peak. The bushes have been dwindling away for some time past, and the pines have been growing thinner in body, fewer in number, smaller in size. A dwarf pine begins to show itself—a scraggly tempest-fighting tree, designed by Nature to grow among the bowlders of the higher peaks and to be the first to stop the slides of snow. The hardy grasses fight beside it, and with them is the little snow-bird, fighting for life too.

Upward, still upward, until great spaces begin to show through the trees and the ground flattens and becomes a floor of rock. In the barrancas on the north side the snow still lies in banks, but on the south side, where the sun falls all day, the ground is bare. You are now above the timber line. Nothing shows but wrecked and shattered strata of rock with patches of

The moun-tain-air.

The dwarf pine.

The summit.

stunted grass. The top is only barren stone.
The uppermost peak, which you have perhaps
seen from the desert a hundred miles away looking like a sharp spine of granite shot up in the
air, turns out to be something more of a dome
than a spine—a rounded knob of gray granite
which you have no difficulty in ascending.

At last you are on the peak and your first
impulse is to look down. But no. Look up! *The look*
You have read and heard many times of the *upward at the sky.*
"deep blue sky." It is a stock phrase in nar-
rative and romance ; but I venture to doubt if
you have ever seen one. It is seen only from
high points—from just such a place as you are
now standing upon. Therefore look up first of
all and see a blue sky that is turning into violet.
Were you ten thousand feet higher in the air
you would see it darkened to a purple-violet
with the stars even at midday shining through
it. How beautiful it is in color and how wonderful it is in its vast reach ! The dome in- *The dark-*
stead of contracting as you rise into it, seems to *blue dome.*
expand. There are no limits to its uttermost
edge, no horizon lines to say where it begins.
It is not now a cup or cover for the world, but
something that reaches to infinity—something
in which the world floats.

And do you notice that the sun is no longer *White light.* yellow but white, and that the light that comes from it is cold with just the faintest shade of violet about it ? The air, too, is changed. Look at the far-away ridges and peaks, some of them snow-capped, but the majority of them bare ; and see the air how blue and purple it looks along the tops and about the slopes. Peak upon peak and chain upon chain disappear to the north and south in a mysterious veil of gray, blue, and purple. Green pine-clad spurs of the peaks, green slopes of the peaks themselves, keep fading away in blue - green mazes and hazes. Look down into the canyons, into the shadowed depths where the air lies packed in a

Distant views. mass, and the top of the mass seems to reflect purple again. This is a very different air from the glowing mockery that dances in the basin of Death Valley. It is mountain-air and yet has something of the sea in it. Even at this height you can feel the sea-breezes moving along

The Pacific. the western slopes. For the ocean is near at hand—not a hundred miles away as the crow flies. From the mountain-top it looks like a flat blue band appended to the lower edge of the sky, and it counts in the landscape only as a strip of color or light.

Between the ocean and the mountain you are standing upon lies the habitable portion of Southern California, spread out like a relief map with its broken ranges, its chaparral-covered foot-hills, and its wide valleys. How fair it looks lying under the westering sun with the shadows drawing in the canyons, and the valleys glowing with the yellow light from fields of ripened barley! And what a contrast to the yellow of the grain are the dark green orchards of oranges and lemons scattered at regular intervals like the squares of a checker-board! And what pretty spots of light and color on the map are the orchards of prunes, apricots, peaches, pears, the patches of velvety alfalfa, the groves of eucalyptus and Monterey cypress, the long waving green lines of cottonwoods and willows that show where run the mountain-streams to the sea!

Southern California.

Yet large as they are, these are only spots. The cultivated portion of the land is but a flower-garden beside the unbroken foot-hills and the untenanted valleys. As you look down upon them the terra-cotta of the granite shows through the chaparral of the hills; and the sands of the valleys have the glitter of the desert. You know intuitively that all this

The garden in the desert.

country was planned by Nature to be desert.
Down to the water-edge of the Pacific she once
carried the light, air, and life of the Mojave
and the Colorado.

But man has in measure changed the desert
conditions by storing the waste waters of the
Reclaiming the valleys. mountains and reclaiming the valleys by irrigation. His success has been phenomenal. Out
of the wilderness there have sprung farms,
houses, towns, cities with their wealth and lux-
ury. But the cultivated conditions are maintained only at the price of eternal vigilance.
Nature is compelled to reap where she has not
sown ; and at times she seems almost human in
the way she rebels and recurs to former conditions. Two, three ; yes, at times, four years
in succession she gives little rain. A great
drouth follows. Then the desert breaks in
upon the valley ranches, upon the fields of barley, the orchards of prunes and peaches and
apricots. Then abandoned farms are quite as
plentiful as in New England ; and once abandoned, but a few years elapse before the desert
has them for its own. Nature is always driven
with difficulty. Out on the Mojave she fights
Fighting fertility. barrenness at every turn ; here in Southern
California she fights fertility. She is deter-

mined to maintain just so much of desert with just so much of its hardy, stubborn life. When she is pleased to enhance it or abate it she will do so ; but in her own good time and way.

Come to the eastern side of the peak and look out once more upon the desert while yet there is time. The afternoon sun is driving its rays through the passes like the sharp-cut shafts of search-lights, and the shadows of the mountains are lengthening in distorted silhouette upon the sands below. Yet still the San Bernardino Range, leading off southeast to the Colorado River, is glittering with sunlight at every peak. You are above it and can see over its crests in any direction. The vast sweep of the Mojave lies to the north ; the Colorado with its old sea-bed lies to the south. Far away to the east you can see the faint forms of the Arizona mountains melting and mingling with the sky ; and in between lie the long pink rifts of the desert valleys and the lilac tracery of the desert ranges.

What a wilderness of fateful buffetings ! All the elemental forces seem to have turned against it at different times. It has been swept by seas, shattered by earthquakes and volcanoes, beaten by winds and sands, and scorched

The desert from the mountain-top.

The great extent of the desert.

The fateful wilderness.

by suns. Yet in spite of all it has endured. It remains a factor in Nature's plan. It maintains its types and out of its desolation it brings forth increase that the species may not perish from the face of the earth.

And yet in the fulness of time Nature designs that this waste and all of earth with it shall perish. Individual, type, and species, all *All shall perish.* shall pass away ; and the globe itself become as desert sand blown hither and yon through space. She cares nothing for the individual man or bird or beast ; can it be thought that she cares any more for the individual world ? She continues the earth-life by the death of the old and the birth of the new; can it be thought that she deals differently with the planetary and stellar life of the universe ? Whence come the new worlds and their satellites unless from the dust of dead worlds compounded with the energy of nebulæ ? Our outlook is limited indeed, but have we not proof in our own moon *The death of worlds.* that worlds do die ? Is it possible that its bleached body will never be disintegrated, will never dissolve and be resolved again into some new life ? And how came it to die ? What was the element that failed—fire, water, or atmosphere ? Perhaps it was water. Perhaps it died through thousands of years with the slow evaporation of moisture and the slow growth of the—desert.

Is then this great expanse of sand and rock the beginning of the end ? Is that the way our globe shall perish ? Who can say ? Nature plans the life, she plans the death ; it must be that she plans aright. For death may be the culmination of all character ; and life but the process of its development. If so, then not in vain these wastes of sand. The harsh destiny, the life-long struggle which they have imposed upon all the plants and birds and animals have been but as the stepping-stones of character. It is true that Nature taxed her invention to the utmost that each might not wage unequal strife. She gave cunning, artifice, persistence, strength ; she wished that each should endure and fulfil to its appointed time. But it is not the armor that develops the wearer thereof. It is the struggle itself—the hard friction of the fight. Not in the spots of earth where plenty breeds indolence do we meet with the perfected type. It is in the land of adversity, and out of much pain and travail that finally emerges the highest manifestation.

Not in vain these wastes of sand. And this

The desert the beginning of the end?

Development through adversity.

time not because they develop character in desert life, but simply because they are beautiful in themselves and good to look upon whether they be life or death. In sublimity—the superlative degree of beauty—what land can equal the desert with its wide plains, its grim mountains, and its expanding canopy of sky! You shall never see elsewhere as here the dome, the pinnacle, the minaret fretted with golden fire at sunrise and sunset; you shall never see elsewhere as here the sunset valleys swimming in a pink and lilac haze, the great mesas and plateaus fading into blue distance, the gorges and canyons banked full of purple shadow. Never again shall you see such light and air and color; never such opaline mirage, such rosy dawn, such fiery twilight. And wherever you go, by land or by sea, you shall not forget that which you saw not but rather felt—the desolation and the silence of the desert.

Sublimity of the waste.

Desolation and silence.

Look out from the mountain's edge once more. A dusk is gathering on the desert's face, and over the eastern horizon the purple shadow of the world is reaching up to the sky. The light is fading out. Plain and mesa are blurring into unknown distances, and mountain-ranges are looming dimly into unknown heights. Warm drifts of lilac-blue are drawn like mists across the valleys ; the yellow sands have shifted into a pallid gray.   The glory of the wilderness has gone down with the sun.   Mystery—that haunting sense of the unknown—is all that remains. It is time that we should say good-night—perhaps a long good-night—to the desert.

*Good-night
to the
desert.*